LIGHTLAB

Lessons for kids to explore the nature of light and to know Jesus

Suzanne O. Shera

Carpenter's Son Publishing

Dedicated to
Noah C., Caroline D., Jesse H., Grace M., Haley G.,
Kellen S., Evi S., and David S., who attended LightLab classes
faithfully and inspired me to prepare this book.

Acknowledgment
This book wouldn't have been possible without a prayer crew,
the children whom I taught, the teachers who tested them,
my children who helped, and my husband, David, who
encouraged me during the entire process.

Copyright © 2017 by Suzanne O. Shera

All rights reserved. No part of this book may be used or reproduced by any means, graphic, electronic, or mechanical, including photocopying, recoding, taping or by an information storage retrieval system without the written permission of the author except in the case of brief quotations embodied in critical articles and reviews.

Published by Carpenter's Son Publishing, Franklin, Tennessee

Published in association with Larry Carpenter of Christian Book Services, LLC

www.christianbookservices.com

Scripture taken from THE HOLY BIBLE, NEW INTERNATIONAL VERSION®, NIV® Copyright © 1973, 1978, 1984, 2011 by Biblica, Inc.™ Used by permission. All rights reserved worldwide.

Scripture quotations are taken from the Holy Bible, New Living Translation, copyright ©1996, 2004, 2007, by Tyndale House Foundation. Used by permission of Tyndale House Publishers, Inc., Carol Stream, Illinois 60188. All rights reserved.

The views expressed in this work are solely those of the author and do not necessarily reflect the views of the publisher, and the publisher hereby disclaims any responsibility for them.

Edited by Robert Irvin

Cover Design by Suzanne Lawing

Interior Design by Adept Content Solutions

ISBN 978-1-942587-83-5

Printed in the United States of America

CONTENTS

Photograph from David Brewster (1855). "Memoirs of the Life, Writings and Discoveries of Sir Isaac Newton, Volume 1" page 46, fig. 7: 38. Public domain. https://commons.wikimedia.org/wiki/File:Newton's reflecting_telescope.jpg

Graphic Art by Christian Schirm: 49. Public domain. https://en.wikipedia.org/wiki/File:Periscope_simple.svg

Wikimedia Commons: 65. CC-PD-Mark. https://commons.wikimedia.org/wiki/File:Snellen06.png

Photo scanned from *The Illustrated History of Colour Photography*, Jack H. Coote: 95. CC-PD-US. https://upload.wikimedia.org/wikipedia/commons/7/7f/Tartan_Ribbon.jpg

Photograph : 95. Public domain. https://en.wikipedia.org/wiki/James_Clerk_Maxwell

Photograph: 39 GFDL free documentation license. https://commons.wikimedia.org/wiki/File%3A.Ancient_Egyptian_mirrors_Louvre.JPG

Graphic Art: 66, 75, © Arizona Board of Regents/ASU Ask a Biologist.

Photos and Graphic design by Suzanne Shera: 4–6, 14, 15 (compass), 24, 31 (tree shadows), 33, 34, 40 (pizza reflection), 41, 42, 48 (last), 49, 50 57, 59, 60, 68, 69, 76 (CD), 77, 78, 84, 86–88, 97, 106–107.

Shutterstock: 67(Phoropter), 93, 104 cover (middle top row). Purchased.

Photograph by Paul Moss at Wellington: 83. Public domain at English Wikipedia. https://commons.wikimedia.org/wiki/File:AuroraAustralisDisplay.jpg

Copyright@The Worlds of David Darling: 85 (color wheel). Used with permission.

WPClipart: 94 (color circles).

Digital Art: www.color-hex.com/color-palette/5642. 95. Used with permission.

Photograph by Betty Wills: 103, Wikimedia Commons, License *CC-BY-SA 4.0.*

NEEDED SUPPLIES FOR LIGHT LAB

SCIENCE STORE
2 Alligator clip wires
1 2.47 Volt bulbs
1 6 V bulb
1 Double Battery Mount
1 Bulb Mount
1 Magnet
1 Compass
2 Mirrors
1 Pair Goggles
1 Magnifying glass
1 Prism
1 DC powered Mini-engine

HOUSEHOLD ITEMS
Adjustable table lamp
2-inch size pictures
Large Metallic spoon
Shoe box
Aluminum Foil
Comb
Opaque Bowl
Water
Shallow 2 cup container
12 oz Jars with different diameters
Strong Myopic glasses
Soap bubbles
a CD
Salt

HARDWARE STORE
1 Ball steel wool (no soap)
1 cup Sand
Flashlight
Strong flashlight

STATIONARY
Metallic paper clips
Plastic covered Paper clips
Binder Clips (Medium Size)
3 x 5 Index Cards
Paper (Various sizes)
Ruler, scissors
Exacto knife
Tape, glue Stick
Twined string
3 inch crayons
Chalk
Pencil
Coloring pencils
Pencils (sharpened)
1 9 V battery
2 1.5 V batteries

INTRODUCTION

Who notices a rainbow or a reflection on a lake without feeling a sense of awe and wonder? When exposed to the unique sceneries created by light, we can't help but share the experience with someone nearby, even if they are strangers! The wondrous effects of light are numerous, and its nature continuously stimulates our curiosity.

Personally, I became fond of light's properties about the time of high school, specifically when I learned about Total Internal Reflection, a phenomenon in which light becomes trapped inside a transparent matter instead of refracting outward, as if it were controlled by a switch. Consequently, I studied Physics and Optics in college, and worked in research for eight years. Soon after I dedicated myself to the Lord Jesus, I noticed the numerous analogies in the Bible about Him being the light of the world. Just as light is an amazing energy and indispensable to the survival of mankind on Earth, Jesus' life on earth is fascinating and He is essential to our relationship with our Father in heaven.

So a desire grew in me to use my knowledge about the nature of Light for God's glory. When an opportunity to minister to fourth and fifth grade children at church opened up in 2008, I developed worksheets about light that included fun hands-on activities and Bible teachings that centered on God's plan for mankind through Jesus. Over the course of a few years, the worksheets evolved to twelve distinct lessons with the following format:

I) **Introduction:** My goal is to present the concept about light and the Bible study theme.

II) **Background:** The scientific concept is explained, including historical overviews, biographies of scientists, especially the Christian practitioners, and modern-day applications.

III) **Activities:** These reinforce the concept and stimulate students' minds in a playful and fun atmosphere.

IV) **God's Light:** This is the Bible study invoked by the concept, followed by questions to reflect on the student's faith and habits.

Throughout the book, teachings on light science and Christianity are sequential and build on the previous chapter to maintain continuity. For example, the scientific concepts are presented in the order of most Optics textbooks, which might discuss:

1. Light sources and its electromagnetic nature (chapters 1, 2)

2. The way light travels in air until obstructed by matter (chapter 3)

3. A close look at shadow formations, reflection, and refraction (chapters 4-8)

4. The splitting of light into colors and recombining them (chapters 9-11)

5. A final activity that uses salty water in a circuit to light a bulb (chapter 12)

The Bible studies revolve around the Gospel message. They are arranged in the following order:

Chapters 1, 2: God's creation of light (Genesis 1:3, 4) and the coming of Jesus as the light of the world was a foretold prophecy, a mystery that eventually unfolded.

Chapters 3, 4: Humans need to understand their sinful nature and their need for a relationship with God.

Chapters 5, 6: Reading God's Word helps to know who God is, how He wants us to live, and how we can enlarge His kingdom.

Chapters 7, 8: It is important to seek God's wisdom and stay focused on Jesus, who is the perfecter of our faith.

Chapter 9: God made many covenants with His people to give them hope. The first covenant was with Noah, and the last, with believers today, is through Jesus.

Chapter 10: As members of one church, we need to be united in serving God and enlarging his kingdom by using our gifts.

Chapter 11: A final retelling of the Gospel message using the colors that symbolize God's character and plan for mankind through Jesus Christ.

Chapter 12: As followers of Jesus, we need to be salt and light so the whole world will know that He is Lord.

Prior to deciding to publish this book, I tested the lessons on eight homeschooled children who attended LightLab classes twice a month. They loved learning about the science of light and were excited by the activities, such as building small circuits, creating sparks, examining shadows, learning magic tricks with reflection and refraction, experimenting with lenses, exploring the properties of white light as it split into the rainbow colors, reversing that same process, combining colors, and more. After engaging in the playful atmosphere that the activities offered, the children listened attentively to the Bible lessons and learned more of God's plan for mankind through Jesus Christ. At our last meeting, the children were able to demonstrate the lessons to their parents, confirming that the teachings were appropriate for their age group.

This book is mainly designed for children eight to eleven years old, and can be used individually as well as in groups. An adult can plan the lessons, supply the items for activities, and minister. It is best to cover a full lesson per session, and these are designed to take up to one and a half hours depending on he size of the group. This group time can be shortened by assigning the Background and God's Light sections to be completed individually before and after.

To add to the group time or assign homework to the children, additional material can be found on the book's website (https://lightlabetc.com). These include: learning assessments, more science activities, projects, photos/videos of the science activities, and links to other resources. A list of vendors to obtain the supplies will be suggested.

The author's wish is that the users of LightLab will be blessed by studies on light, which God created first for the world. As children marvel in the nature of light, they will delight in Jesus, who reflects God's light and calls them to the Father. They will also learn of the Holy Spirit's role to guide and show them how to shine God's light on others.

JOHN 8:12

When Jesus spoke again to the people, he said, "I am **the light of the world.** *Whoever follows me will never walk in darkness, but will have* **the light of** *life."*

CHAPTER ONE

LET THERE BE LIGHT!

INTRODUCTION

In the Bible there are nearly three hundred references to light, the first one in Genesis 1:3, 4.

> And God said, "Let there be **light**," and there was **light**.
> God saw that the **light** was good, and he separated
> the **light** from the **darkness**.

Light is often mentioned in the Bible as a blessing from the Lord because it separates us from darkness. God also created the moon, the sun, and other stars to give light and maintain

1

life on earth. In this lesson, we will review the importance of sunlight, test objects that conduct electricity, and have fun creating it. Then we will discuss how light guided the people of the Bible and why Jesus is called the Light of the World.

BACKGROUND

The light sources of the universe consist of the stars, the sun being the closest and most important for Earth. The sun is still 93 million miles away, a perfect distance to keep our Earth warm enough. If the sun were a little closer, the oceans would dry up. If the sun were further away, its heat would not be enough and everything would freeze!

The sun looks small when we look at it from far, but it is actually so big it could hold a million earths inside it! The other stars look smaller than the sun because their distance from earth is much larger. We also see them only at night because the sun's brightness during the day is too powerful.

Light is known to travel faster than anything in the world, at a speed of about 186,000 miles per second (300,000 km/sec). For example, it takes sunlight about 8 minutes to reach the Earth, and only 1.3 seconds to travel from the moon to Earth! If we could travel at the speed of light, we would go around the Earth 7.5 times in one second!

Light is very important for life because it provides the energy needed to make plants grow through a process called photosynthesis (*photo* = light; *synthesis* = put together). Plants need sunlight to mix the water they absorb from the ground with the carbon dioxide they inhale from the air.

2

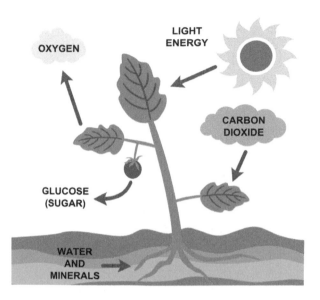

Their reaction produces sugar for the growth of plants, and oxygen is released into the air.

At nighttime, throughout our history on Earth, people have relied on different sources of light, such as torches, oil lamps, and candles until the generation of electricity. Thomas Edison was credited for designing the

electric light bulb in 1879, and these were used for a century after many modifications. The Tungsten wire inside the bulb glows as electric current flows through the filament inside and heats it up. Those bulbs use a lot of energy and are being replaced by more efficient light sources such as fluorescent and LED bulbs.

ACTIVITIES

The following activities will show how electricity flows through conducting materials to light a bulb. You will test materials that are conductors (they let electricity flow), and insulators (these prevent the flow of electricity). Then you will watch a piece of steel glow and burn.

1) LIGHT ON/OFF

Need: 2.4 Volt small bulb in a mount, 2 mounted batteries, Alligator clip wires, and small test items: metallic, plastic, wood, etc.

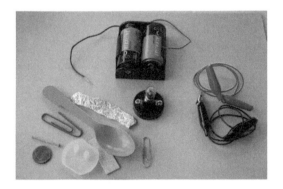

1. Clip the two alligators on the metallic screws bulb mounts.
2. Connect free ends of alligator wires to mounted battery wires to test if the bulb turns on.

3. Separate one battery wire from one alligator and place the test items between them one at a time. Observe if the bulb light goes on or stays off.

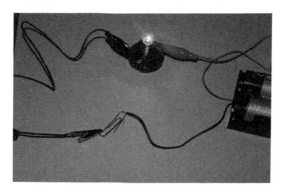

4. Separate the **conductors**, items which turn on the light bulb, from the insulators, items which do not turn the light bulb on. Record the results below:

   Conductors: _____

   Insulators: _____

5. Now place all the <u>conducting</u> items in series, making sure they touch each other. Watch light bulb go ON again!

2) LIGHT GLOW

Need: Two 1.5 Volt batteries in holders, two alligator wires, small non-flammable container filled with sand, soap-free steel wool, and goggles.

1. Pull a string of steel wool and grip 1 cm between two alligator wires, laying all on top of a sand box.

2. Connect one battery wire to a free alligator, and put on your goggles.

3. Connect the last free alligator to the other battery wire, while you watch the steel.

4. The steel string should glow and break.

5. *DISCONNECT BATTERY WIRE FROM ALLIGATOR* before you repeat.

GOD'S LIGHT

We know that light is important for our existence and an exciting energy to explore. Remember: God made light, and He liked it.

1. Read **1 John 1:5, 6** to explore why it is said that "God is light."

This is the message we have heard from him and declare to you: God is light; in him there is no darkness at all. If we claim to have fellowship with him and yet walk in the darkness, we lie and do not live out the truth.

- Is there any darkness in light? _____
- Circle which shows the truth: darkness / light

Since there can be no darkness in light, light is perfect. That is why God is said to be light and is therefore holy and pure. God is also reliable, and reveals to us the true way.

2. Read **Psalm 18:28**.

You, Lord, keep my lamp burning; my God turns my darkness into light.

- Who can turn our darkness to light? _____
- What does darkness in us represent? _____

Light is indeed more powerful than darkness, just as God is more powerful than the sin in our hearts.

3. Read **John 8:12** to see who will help us walk in the Light.

When Jesus spoke again to the people, he said, "I am the light of the world. Whoever follows me will never walk in darkness, but will have the light of life."

- How does Jesus describe himself? _____
- What does Jesus promise? _____

There were about 400 prophecies bout Jesus coming to the world, an event we celebrate yearly during Christmas with lights and presents. This prophecy was revealed to the Magi (wise men), who traveled thousands of miles to find Jesus. The story is told in **Matthew 2:1-11.**

4. Read **Matthew 2:1-2.**

After Jesus was born in Bethlehem in Judea, during the time of King Herod, Magi from the east came to Jerusalem and asked, "Where is the one who has been born king of the Jews? We saw his star when it rose and have come to worship him."

- What guided the Magi? _____
- Who was the star leading to? _____
- What did the Magi want to do? _____

The region's king, Herod, was disturbed and wanted to know where the prophets said this king would be born? His advisers quoted the prophet Micah, who said, 700 years earlier, that the child would be born in Bethlehem. So King Herod sent the Magi there and asked them to report back and tell him the location of the child.

5. Read **Matthew 2:9-11.**

After they had heard the king, they went on their way, and the star they had seen when it rose went ahead of them until it stopped over the place where the child was. When they saw the star, they were overjoyed. On coming to the house, they saw the child with his mother Mary, and they bowed down and worshiped him. Then they opened their treasures and presented him with gifts of gold, frankincense and myrrh.

- How did the Magi feel when they saw the guiding star?

  _____

- What did they first do when they saw him?

  _____

- What did they give him? _____

Guided by a star, the Magi traveled thousands of miles to worship the Great King of the Jews. No one but God can fulfill a prophecy such as this one!

6. Finally, read what the disciple Peter said in **2 Peter 1:19**.

*We also have the prophetic message as something completely reliable, and you will do well to pay attention to it, as to a **light** shining in a dark place, until the day dawns and the morning star rises in your hearts.*

- How did Peter describe the prophetic message?

  _____

- How should we treat it? _____
- What is the prophetic message similar to?

  _____

- Who does he refer to by "the morning star"?

  _____

Christmas is, therefore, an opportunity to pay attention to the time Jesus was born. Since it happens during the winter, when the days are short, we appreciate more lights around us. Just as Christmas lights add joy and warmth to our winter nights, Jesus lights up our lives and leads us to the Father.

REFLECTIONS

- Do you prefer to walk in the light or the darkness?

  _____

- What are your thoughts about Jesus so far?

  _____

MEMORY VERSE: JOHN 8:12

When Jesus spoke again to the people, he said, "I am the light of the world. Whoever follows me will never walk in darkness, but will have the light of life.

CHAPTER TWO

WHAT IS THIS LIGHT?

INTRODUCTION

We all agree light is an extremely important part of our lives; we can't survive without it. But what *is it* exactly? We will learn how light is created; we will explore Electricity (E) and Magnetism (M), and conclude that light is an EM wave!

Then we will discuss how Jesus was a mystery for the longest time, as early as Genesis. When He finally revealed Himself to the world, many acknowledged Him as their savior and spread the Good News to all generations ahead!

BACKGROUND

The nature of light was a complete mystery until the 18th century, when scientists began experimenting with it. Some of the experiments indicated that light consisted of particles, and others pointed out that it was wave-like. After a long debate, scientists agreed that light had a dual property; it behaved as a particle *and* a wave. The light particles, called photons, travel like waves!

These photons are energy particles released by electrons inside an atom. The diagram describes an atom with its nucleus in the center. The electrons revolve around the nucleus in circular paths called orbits. The electrons with more energy occupy the outer orbits. When an electron gets excited, it moves to a higher orbit. When it returns to its home orbit, it releases its gained energy in the form of heat and light.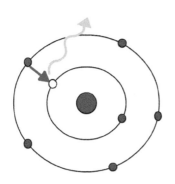

People have also been curious about *Electricity* and *Magnetism*, which were believed to be separate from each other. It was not until the 1800s that scientists found a *connection* between Electricity and Magnetism. This new science was called *Electro-Magnetism*. Hans Christian Oersted was the first to discover that an electric current causes a magnet to move. Two other scientists, who were devout Christians, made important discoveries in *Electromagnetism*, as well as in *Light*:

Michael Faraday (1791-1867) was one of the greatest experimentalists, and is mostly known for inventing the dynamo (an electric generator). He discovered that a moving magnet causes electricity to flow in a conducting wire. This led to the building of power plants that push electrons to your lightbulbs, computers, and even phones. Faraday also was intrigued by light's nature and predicted that it was related to electricity and magnetism.

James Clerk Maxwell (1831-1879) was fond of Faraday because of his discoveries and his faith. Maxwell used his extensive knowledge in mathematics to verify that light was indeed electric and magnetic in nature, just as Faraday had observed! Maxwell's discovery was essential to the development of today's modern technology: motors, television, computers, home electronics, and much more.

13

ACTIVITIES

We will first explore magnetism as we test this property in various items, and we'll observe the attraction between magnetic poles. Then we will work with electromagnetism and see for ourselves how flowing electricity indicates the presence of a magnetic field.

MAGNETIC OR NOT

Need: *magnet, the same items you used for the conductivity test*

1. Test all items with a magnet and note whether they were attracted or not.

2. Record the list of:

Magnetic: _____

Non-magnetic _____

Are some items conductive but not magnetic? _____

COMPASS EFFECT

Need: *12" electric wire, battery in holder, compass*

1. Wrap the wire from its middle around the compass twice, making sure that N is on the side (as shown).

2. Tape it firmly on the back of the compass and let it settle on a table so the needle points you to North (N).

3. Connect the battery wires to the alligator clips, and watch the compass needle. What happens to the compass needle? _____

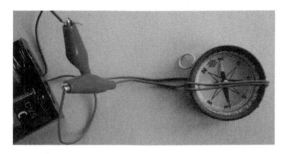

4. Switch the alligator clips to the other battery wires. What do you observe now?

_____

This is how Oersted showed that when electricity flows in a wire, it affects the magnet of a compass. He concluded, therefore, that wherever there is an electric current, there must also be a magnetic force. Faraday was able to prove the reverse by moving a magnet inside a wire loop and causing electricity to flow. Faraday also predicted that light must be related to electricity and magnetism. When he mentioned this during his 1846 lectures at the Royal Institution in London, everyone made fun of him.

Maxwell, born 40 years after Faraday, had faith in his prediction. He also admired Faraday, as we have said, for his intellect and faith. Maxwell proved that Faraday's prediction was correct, and he explained, mathematically, how light is an energy that moves forward in pulses with electric and magnetic components.

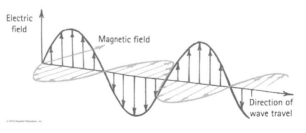

GOD'S LIGHT

Just like the nature of light, Christ also was a mystery to those around Him. They couldn't tell who He was! Some were attracted to Him, while others accused Him of lying and blasphemy.

1. Read **John 7:11, 12.**

Now at the festival the Jewish leaders were watching for Jesus and asking, "Where is he?" Among the crowds there was widespread whispering about him. Some said, "He is a good man." Others replied, "No, he deceives the people."

- What kind of a man did the people think Jesus was?

_____ _____

2. Read **Matthew 16:13-17.**

When Jesus came to the region of Caesarea Philippi, he asked his disciples, "Who do people say the Son of Man is?" They replied, "Some say John the Baptist; others say Elijah; and still others, Jeremiah or one of the prophets." "But what about you?" he asked. "Who do you say I am?" Simon Peter answered, "You are the Messiah, the Son of the living God." Jesus replied, "Blessed are you, Simon son of Jonah, for this was not revealed to you by flesh and blood, but by my Father in heaven."

- Who did these people think Jesus was (v. 14)?

_____ _____

_____ _____

- Who did Peter say Jesus was (v. 16)?

_____

- Who revealed that to Peter?

_____

3. Read **Colossians 1:26-27**

The mystery that has been kept hidden for ages and generations, but is now disclosed to the Lord's people. To them God has chosen to make known among the Gentiles the glorious riches of this mystery, which is Christ in you, the hope of glory.

- To who is the hidden mystery of Christ revealed?

_____

The ones who listened to him and stayed with him until the end finally understood that He was their hope and the *Way* to the Father. They received him as their Savior and enjoyed their fellowship with him.

4. Read **Hebrews 1:1-3** to know more about Jesus.

In the past God spoke to our ancestors through the prophets at many times and in various ways, but in these last days he has spoken to us by his Son, whom he appointed heir of all things, and through whom also he made the universe. The Son is the radiance of God's glory and the exact representation of his being, sustaining all things by his powerful word. After he had provided purification for sins, he sat down at the right hand of the Majesty in heaven.

- Who did God appoint heir of all things?

_____

- What did he make through him?

_____

- What does Christ radiate?

_____

- Who can purify us from our sins?

_____

5. Read **2 Corinthians 4:5, 6.**

For what we preach is not ourselves, but Jesus Christ as Lord, and ourselves as your servants for Jesus' sake. For God, who said, "Let light shine out of darkness," made his light shine in our hearts to give us the light of the knowledge of God's glory displayed in the face of Christ.

- Who should we preach about?
  _____ not _____

- Where does God's light shine?
  _____

- What does it give us?
  _____

- Who displays that light?
  _____

Read below what the two scientists referenced in this chapter, Michael Faraday and James Maxwell, shared about how their scientific discoveries deepened their faith in Christ.

"And therefore, brethren, we ought to value the privilege of knowing God's truth far beyond anything we can have in this world. The more we see the perfection of God's law fulfilled in Christ, the more we ought to thank God for His unspeakable gift."

—Michael Faraday

"The more we enter into Christ's work He will have more room to work His work in us. For He always desires to

he one with us. Our worship is social, and Christ will be where two or three are gathered together in His name."

—James C. Maxwell

- What did Michael Faraday value more than anything in the world?

  _____

- What did James Maxwell say Christ's desire was?

  _____

REFLECTIONS

- Who is Christ to you?

  _____

- What new things did you learn about Jesus Christ?

  _____

MEMORY VERSE: 2 CORINTHIANS 4:6

For God, who said, "Let light shine out of darkness," made his light shine in our hearts to give us the light of the knowledge of God's glory displayed in the face of Christ.

CHAPTER THREE

LET THE LIGHT THROUGH!

INTRODUCTION

When God created us in His image (Genesis 1:27), He gave us a sense of wonder about His creation. Read Psalm 19:1.

The heavens declare the glory of God;
the skies proclaim the work of his hands..

Astronomers study the universe with the help of telescopes, revealing to us magnificent views of stars and planets. One of the most popular National Aeronautics and Space Administration (NASA) images captured by the Hubble Telescope is named the Pillars of Creation, which shows star formations in a region of the Eagle Nebula. In this lesson, we will understand how light travels in space and what happens when it is blocked. Then we will discover how we can be influenced by God's light—if we come to him just as we are.

BACKGROUND

While light from the sun takes 8 minutes to reach earth, light from various stars travels for years until the photons reach our eyes. For example, light from the closest star system, Alpha Centauri, takes 4 1/2 years to reach our planet Earth! This is after it has traveled 25 trillion miles! Therefore, light can travel very long distances in space in the same direction without fading—unless something gets in its way.

For example, Earth and the moon are both opaque because they are made of rocky and dense materials. Therefore, they block sunlight and cause the solar and lunar eclipses. During a solar eclipse, the moon is on the same plane between the sun and Earth. Therefore, the sun is blocked and the moon's shadow is cast on earth. Those living

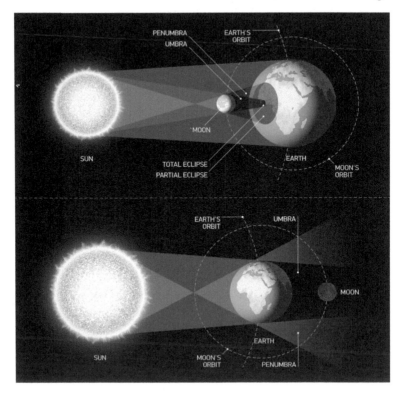

on that spot of Earth will stop seeing the sun for a couple minutes, because both moon and Earth are moving. During a lunar eclipse, our Earth that blocks sunlight from the moon. Its shadow is cast on the moon, and our orbiting moon is obscured for several minutes.

The Earth's atmosphere is composed of various gases and small particles, yet it is clear enough to allow most of the visible sunlight through. Although we still see objects in space through the transparent atmosphere, they appear differently than if we were to observe them straight from space. On

a cloudy day, the sky is no longer visible and the amount of light that gets through depends on the thickness of the clouds. Opaque clouds are thick and dark, and they block the sun completely. Translucent clouds are thinner and they allow more light from the sun to come through.

There are objects all around us that affect the passage of light in different ways depending on whether they are opaque, transparent, or translucent. Opaque objects stop light completely and block the view from the other side. Translucent objects allow some light through, but

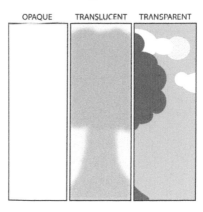

OPAQUE   TRANSLUCENT   TRANSPARENT

allow an unclear view of the other side. Transparent objects let light through and allow a clear view of the other side.

ACTIVITIES

Let's see for ourselves that light travels straight, and then determine whether the objects around us are transparent, opaque, or translucent.

THE PATH OF LIGHT

Need: three 3x5 index cards, a ruler, sharp pencil, three large binder clips, flashlight

Procedure:

1. Pierce a hole through the center of the three index cards at the same time with with the sharpened end of a pencil.

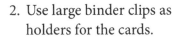

2. Use large binder clips as holders for the cards.

3. Turn your flashlight on, and hold it horizontally behind the first card at the same height as hole, so that your partner sees the light travel through it from the other side.

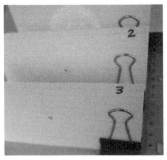

4. Add one and then two cards, one at a time, using the ruler, and check to see that light goes through the holes to the other side.

5. At this point, all holes should be aligned with the light beam. Your eye should see the light beam through card 3 from the other side.

6. Try to move the second card sideways by a half-inch as you look through card 3. Do you still see the light beam? _____

As soon as you move cards 1 or 2, the light will disappear because it doesn't move on a zig zag path, seeking the holes. Suppose you slip a string through the three holes. If you move either card, the string also will move. But not so with light!

DESCRIBE THE OBJECTS
Using the same principles and shining your flashlight, describe the objects in the left column with a √ mark.

Objects to test	Opaque	Transparent	Translucent
glass			
wood			
air			
tissue paper			
water			
black construction paper			
Choose something to try!			

GOD'S LIGHT

People are sometimes described as "transparent" or "opaque." A transparent person is comfortable talking about himself or herself, flaws and all. An opaque person hides their thoughts and feelings from others. Some people are a little of both, depending on where they are and who they are with. It is good if everyone has someone with whom they can be transparent. Otherwise, we will feel lonely because we are hiding all the time, and nobody understands how we are feeling and what our problems are.

Let's study some Bible passages to understand what it's like to be transparent with God, who wants us to come to him just as we are. We'll see that being humble about the truth of our hearts will indeed set us free.

1. Read **Proverbs 28:13.**

   Whoever conceals his sins does not prosper, but the one who confesses and renounces them finds mercy.

   • What happens to the one who hides their sins from God?

   _____

   • What happens to the person who confesses and renounces their sins?

   _____

King David was called "a man after God's own heart" because he walked closely with Him and trusted Him at all times. He understood how weak and sinful he was, yet how merciful God was.

2. Read **Psalm 32:3-5;** King David expressed some of his deepest thoughts to God.

When I kept silent,
my bones wasted away
through my groaning all day long.

For day and night
your hand was heavy on me;
my strength was sapped
as in the heat of summer.

Then I acknowledged my sin to you
and did not cover up my iniquity.
I said, "I will confess
my transgressions to the Lord."
And you forgave the guilt of my sin.

- How was King David feeling?

  _____

- When did God forgive him?

  _____

When he realized he made a mistake, David felt deep sorrow—and felt remorse for his sin. He asked God's forgiveness, and God had mercy on him.

3. Read **Luke 18:9-14**, the Parable of the Pharisee and the Tax Collector.

To some who were confident of their own righteousness and looked down on everyone else, Jesus told this parable: "Two men went up to the temple to pray, one a Pharisee and the other a tax collector. The Pharisee stood by himself and prayed: 'God, I thank you that I am not like other people— robbers, evildoers, adulterers—or even like this tax collector. I fast twice a week and give a tenth of all I get.'

"But the tax collector stood at a distance. He would not even look up to heaven, but beat his breast and said, 'God, have mercy on me, a sinner.'

"I tell you that this man, rather than the other, went home justified before God. For all those who exalt themselves will be humbled, and those who humble themselves will be exalted."

- To whom did Jesus tell this parable?

  _____

- Who was humble, the Pharisee or tax collector?

  _____

- Who did God justify, the Pharisee or tax collector?

  _____

4. Read this portion of **2 Corinthians 12:9.**

   Therefore I will boast all the more gladly about my weaknesses, so that Christ's power may rest on me.

- Does God want us to boast about our weaknesses or our strengths? _____

- What does Christ give us then?

  _____!

5. Read **James 5:16.**

   Confess your sins to each other and pray for each other so that you may be healed. The prayer of a righteous man is powerful and effective.

As Christians, God wants us to be transparent with others too, and to _____ for one another. That is why He gave us a family, friends, and the church.

REFLECTIONS

- Did you know that God wants you to come to him just as you are? _____

- Are you willing to humbly confess your sins?

  _____

- What have you learned about God's character so far?

  _____

  _____

MEMORY VERSE: 2 CORINTHIANS 12:9

Therefore I will boast all the more gladly about my weaknesses, so that Christ's power may rest on me.

CHAPTER FOUR

HOW BIG IS YOUR SHADOW?

INTRODUCTION

God created the celestial bodies not only to give light to Earth, but to tell time as well. Read Genesis 1:14.

And God said, "Let there be lights in the vault of the sky to separate the day from the night, and let them serve as signs to mark sacred times and days and years."

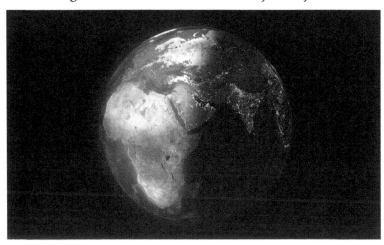

Ancient civilizations indeed relied on the phases of the moon and the sun's location to tell the time of day and year. In this lesson, we will learn about the history of measuring time, and we will explore shadows. Then we will examine ourselves next to God's light and discuss the importance of staying close to Him.

BACKGROUND

Since light travels along a straight line, it will stop when obstructed by opaque objects, because, as we learned in the last chapter, it can't travel around or through such an object. Therefore, it forms a shadow on the other side of the object. The shadow's color is black because light is absent. The shadow shows the shape of the object, but no other details. The shape of a shadow will change in size depending on the distance and angle of light from the object.

For example, the shadows that the sun casts will change throughout the day, as the sun rises from the east and sets in the west. The shadow of an object will be longest at sunrise and sunset, when the angle the sun forms with the horizon is the smallest. At noon, however, the sun is high in the sky—essentially, 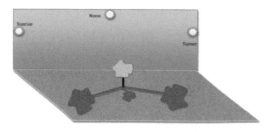 straight above us—and the shadow will be the shortest when the angle the sun forms with the horizon is largest.

Ancient civilizations studied the shifting of shadows from the sun to tell time. The Babylonians built an obelisk similar to this country's Washington Monument. The Egyptians built the first sundial, and the Greeks used geometry to build more complex ones.

In 100 A.D. sundials used the gnomon, which is a tilted axis parallel to the Earth axis, to enable the shadows to always point to the same spot at the same time each day throughout the year. Even after mechanical watches were invented in the 14th century, sundials were still a popular addition to gardens and public centers.

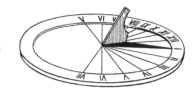

The phases of our moon are also due to its different location during its orbit around Earth, and they depend on the angle of sun-Earth-moon. The visible section of the moon is the one facing the sun and its dark section is the part facing away from the sun. The phases of the moon repeat in a 28-day cycle, which is the period of time it takes the moon to go around the earth.

Many ancient civilizations based their calendar on the phases of the moon; thus, they developed the lunar calendar. Since 1582 A.D., the Gregorian Calendar has been introduced and adopted by most nations until today. This is a solar calendar, which follows Earth's orbit around the sun. It is 365 and 1/4 days, which is why we have a leap year every four years, when the month of February has 29 days instead of 28.

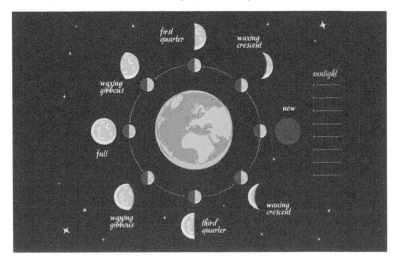

ACTIVITIES

One can have so much fun with shadows! A few activities here will help you create them indoors and outdoors. You will also evaluate their size based on their location relative to the light source.

OUTDOOR SHIFTING SHADOWS

Need: Sunny day, chalk

1. Stand on ground where you can see your shadow.
2. Measure the length of your shadow.
3. Trace your feet first, and have your partner trace the shadow of your body on the ground.
4. Go out again every hour and stand exactly where your feet were the first time.
5. Measure again; record your results below.

Date: Time of day								
Length of your shadow								

- What happens to your shadow as the sun moves?

INDOOR SHIFTING SHADOWS

Need: Adjustable desk lamp, large white paper, ruler, index card, scissors, binder clip

1. Cut the index card in the general shape of a person and use the binder clip as stand.

2. Lay the sheet of paper on a table or floor.

3. Put the person-shaped card at the edge of the sheet.

4. Place the lamp directly over it such that a shadow is not seen.

5. Holding the lamp in the same spot, move the person along a straight line away from the lamp.

6. Record the shadow's length (L), in centimeters (cm), at various distances of your Card Man from the starting point.

Distance of Card Man; distance in cm	5	10	15	20	25	30	35	40
Shadow length; length in cm								

- When Card Man is closest to the light, the size of the shadow is

  _____ .

- As Card Man is moved farther from the light, the size of the shadow

  a. increases _____

  b. decreases _____

There are many more fun games you can play with shadows!

GOD'S LIGHT

Suppose the card man is one of us, the light is Jesus, and the shadow represents our sins and troubles. Maybe we lost someone close to us, a friend has wronged us, we cheated on a test, or we hurt another person.

1. Read **Isaiah 59:9-12** to see how Isaiah felt one particular day.

> **(9)** *So justice is far from us,*
> *and righteousness does not reach us.*
> *We look for light, but all is darkness;*
> *for brightness, but we walk in deep shadows.*

> **(10)** *Like the blind we grope along the wall,*
> *feeling our way like people without eyes.*
> *At midday we stumble as if it were twilight;*
> *among the strong, we are like the dead.*

> **(11)** *We all growl like bears;*
> *we moan mournfully like doves.*
> *We look for justice, but find none;*
> *for deliverance, but it is far away.*

> **(12)** *For our offenses are many in your sight,*
> *and our sins testify against us.*
> *Our offenses are ever with us,*
> *and we acknowledge our iniquities*

Answer the following questions and indicate the verses that support your answer.

- Do the people feel treated fairly?
  _____ Verse _____
- Where do they feel like they are walking?
  _____ Verse _____
- Do they have clear vision?
  _____ Verse _____

35

- The people feel far from God because they committed too many _____ and _____ .
  Verse _____

- Did the people finally repent?
  _____ Verse _____

- In the previous lesson, we saw that the Lord rewards the people who repent and are humbled. That is why the Lord had mercy on the sufferings of His people and promised them a Redeemer (Isaiah 59:20).

"The Redeemer will come to Jerusalem to buy back those in Israel who have turned from their sins," says the LORD (**NLT**).

2. Read **Luke 1:76-79**, a passage by Zechariah, the father of John the Baptist, who prophesied about Jesus, our Redeemer.

*"And you, my child, will be called a prophet of the **Most High**;*
for you will go on before the Lord to prepare the way for him,
to give his people the knowledge of salvation
through the forgiveness of their sins,
*because of the tender **mercy** of our God,*
by which the rising sun will come to us from heaven to
*shine on those living in **darkness** and in the **shadow***
*of death, to **guide** our **feet** into the **path** of **peace**."*

- His child John will be called the prophet of the
  _____ _____ .

- Zechariah says God will forgive our sins because He is
  _____ .

- Where did the rising sun come from?
  _____

- Who will it shine upon?
  _____

God the Father sent his Son Jesus to be the light that saves us from darkness and shows us peace. In the activity, remember how Card Man's shadow got smaller the closer he was to the lamp? Our troubles and sins will also be smaller the closer we are to Christ.

3. Read **James 1:17**.

*Every good **and** perfect gift is from above, coming down from the Father of the heavenly **lights**, who does not change like shifting **shadows**.*

- How is the gift of light we receive from Jesus? _____ and _____
- Does He change? _____

So, let us do everything possible to stay near Him instead of wandering in darkness. His will is perfect, and He wants to reveal it to His children.

REFLECTIONS

- Do you sometimes feel like your troubles are many?

  _____

- Are there habits or character issues you have a hard time controlling?

  _____

- Have you tried to talk to God about them? If so, describe your efforts.

  _____

MEMORY VERSE: JAMES 1:17

*Every good **and** perfect gift is from above, coming down from the Father of the heavenly **lights**, who does not change like shifting **shadows**.*

CHAPTER FIVE

WHAT DO YOU SEE?

INTRODUCTION

Do you know a household that doesn't have a single mirror? The answer is probably not. We use them every day—to check our face, hair, and clothes. We also use them in cars for safety and guidance. Mirrors are used in telescopes to gaze at the heavens, as well as in many industrial applications. In this lesson, we will learn some of the history of mirrors, understand how they are made, and we'll create some interesting reflections. Then we will discuss how the Bible acts as the mirror that reflects God's Word to us, and shows us His plan for mankind through Christ.

BACKGROUND

When man first saw his reflection in a pond, it was probably considered some sort of magic; later, he understood exactly what he was seeing. The first manmade mirrors were manufactured thousands of years ago by ancient civilizations in Egypt, China, Etruria,

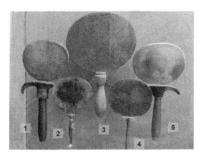

Anatolia, and Greece. Sheets of metals (copper, silver, bronze, gold) were flattened and polished to create mirrors. The mirrors in the photo are from Egypt (1600 B.C. and older). In the Bible, there is mention of such ancient mirrors. We read this when Moses was leading the Jews out of Egypt (Exodus 38:8).

They made the bronze basin and its bronze stand from the mirrors of the women who served at the entrance to the tent of meeting.

In the first century B.C., around the same time as the founding of the Roman Empire, glassblowing was invented in Lebanon. Soon after, the first mirrors were made by applying a layer of molten metal to flattened glass. Throughout the centuries that would follow, manufacturing techniques improved, producing flat mirrors with smooth, reflective coatings.

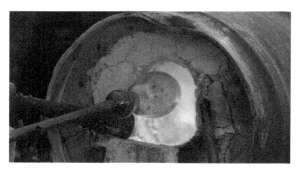

Today, affordable mirrors for home use are made in factories, but the ones used in technology can cost thousands of dollars. The cost depends on the type of metallic coating (aluminum, silver, gold) and the method used to produce the mirror. Basically, the flatter the surface of the glass and the smoother the metallic coating, the greater the reflection quality. For example, mirrors used to reflect laser lights require expensive polishing machines; these are coated with silver or gold inside vacuum evaporation chambers.

When light shines on an object, it bounces off in many directions. If a mirror is nearby, the light rays that reach it reflect back to the eyes. The reflection seems to be coming from the other side of the mirror, as the dashed rays in the picture indicate. This image is not real, nor can it be touched, but it does tell us exactly how the object looks!

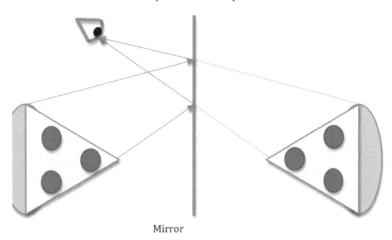

Mirror

ACTIVITIES

Perform a series of fun activities to form reflections that complete, multiply, and deform an object.

MULTIPLE REFLECTIONS

Need: 2 mirrors, pictures cut in symmetrical halves (for example a face, a heart), Cut in quarters (round pie, pizza, square box), 3" pencils or crayons, a small object

1. Use one mirror to make the halved pictures whole again. Check when done: ☐

2. Use the two mirrors to make the pictures in quarters whole again. Check when done: ☐

3. Use two mirrors and two 3" pencils or crayons. Put two mirrors next to each other, forming an angle, and then use one or two crayons and their reflections to create the different shapes as you change the angle. Draw the shapes you see:

A triangle:	A square:

A pentagon:	A hexagon:

4. Use two mirrors and a small object.

   a. Face two mirrors toward each other, leaving about six inches in between.

   b. Put an object in between and look into one mirror.

   c. How many images can you count? _____

FUNNY REFLECTIONS

Need: Large polished metallic spoons

Look at your reflection from both sides of the spoon. Describe your image when you see:

   1. The side curved toward you (the term for this is *convex*):

   _____

   2. The side curved away from you (the term for this is *concave*): _____

GOD'S LIGHT

When we see ourselves in a mirror, we don't quickly forget our face. We remember all our features: the shape of our face, the color of our eyes, and more. The mirror also tells us if we look presentable, or whether we need to wash up, comb our hair, etc.

- Do you ignore your dirty face when you see it in the mirror? _____
- What do you do?

  _____

- Why?

  _____

In the same way, when we read the Bible, we see how God wants us to live. If we ignore what we read, we sin and need to repent to have peace.

1. Read what James tells us in **James 1:22-25**.

Do not merely listen to the word, and so deceive yourselves. Do what it says. Anyone who listens to the word but does not do what it says is like someone who looks at his face in a mirror and, after looking at himself, goes away and immediately forgets what he looks like. But whoever looks intently into the perfect law that gives freedom, and continues in it—not forgetting what they have heard, but doing it—they will be blessed in what they do.

- Is it enough to listen to the Word of God? _____
- What else should we do?

  _____

- What is James comparing the Word of God to?

  _____

- What will happen to those who don't forget God's Word and do it?

_____

The Bible, therefore, is like a reflection of God. It allows us to check whether our thoughts and actions are in agreement with His will. His Word is true and clear, and it tells us if we need to change our ways. When we read and obey what God says in His Word, we will be blessed, because God's ways are perfect.

2. Now let's discuss the word *reflect*. The apostle Paul used this word in **2 Timothy 2:7**.

> *"**Reflect** on what I am saying, for the Lord will give you insight into all this."*

- What does Paul mean by reflect?

_____

- Who will give us insight?

_____

The Word of God also says that Christ alone is perfect, for He was God himself who came to the world for us, sinners. He alone obeyed His Father completely, even dying for all the wrong we have done. You might ask why Jesus had to die to forgive our sins? Let's read on.

3. Read **Romans 3:23** to see what Paul says about this.

*For all have **sinned** and have fallen short of the glory of God.*

- Do only a few sin? How many have sinned? _____
- Are we ever good enough for God? _____

All of us sin, and deserve to be punished. The punishment is separation from God. In the times before Jesus, the Jews had to go to the priests of the Temple and sacrifice an animal to receive forgiveness for their sins. The process was very complicated, and offered only temporary covering of the sins. God promised the Messiah, who would deliver His people from their sins for eternity.

4. Read **John 1:29** to learn what John the Baptist said about Jesus.

The next day John saw Jesus coming toward him and said, "Look, the Lamb of God, who takes away the sin of the world!"

- What was the Lamb of God going to do?

_____

Jesus was the Messiah who was going to be sacrificed for our sins, like a perfect lamb.

5. Read **Hebrews 10:10.**

And by that will, we have been made holy through the sacrifice of the body of Jesus Christ **once for all.**

- How many times did Jesus have to be sacrificed?

_____

6. Read **1 Corinthians 15:4** to learn what happened to Jesus after his death.

*"... that he was buried, that he was raised on the third day **according to** the **Scriptures** ... "*

After his death, Christ was glorified with His resurrection, and He appeared to many, giving them hope for the future.

If God is showing your sin, Jesus alone can take it away. God did this because of His great love for us, and His desire is to spend eternity with us. Trusting Jesus as your Savior is the most important decision of your life.

REFLECTIONS

- Do you understand that your sins need forgiven?

  _____

- Do you feel a need for Jesus to take your sins away?

  _____

- Have you trusted Jesus as your Savior?

  _____

MEMORY VERSE: ROMANS 5:8

*But God **demonstrates** his own love for us in this:*
While we were still sinners, Christ died for us.

CHAPTER SIX

REFLECT HIS LIGHT!

INTRODUCTION

We are nearly halfway through our journey in Lightlab! So far, we have created light with a circuit, understood that it is electromagnetic, tracked its path, and explored shadows and reflections. Also, we learned that God created light, and mankind, to whom he revealed the mystery in Jesus, the light of the world. Jesus desires that we stay transparent, He draws us near to Himself, and He makes us closer to His image. In this lesson, we'll take another look at reflection, and we'll learn how periscopes work. Then we will describe how a follower of Christ can enjoy His fellowship and share His joy with the rest of the world.

BACKGROUND

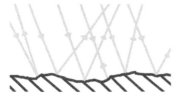

When light hits a surface, some of it bounces back and some gets absorbed. If the surface is rugged, the light will bounce back in various directions, as shown in this figure. You see that the incoming rays that point in the same direction get reflected without any order. The reflection of the object, therefore, will be blurry.

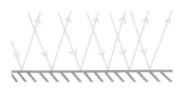

On the other hand, if the surface is smooth, like that of a mirror, all light rays will reflect back in order. The incoming rays are easily traced after their reflection because all the rays stay parallel. This is why a pond gives a good image only when it is still. When there are ripples, however, the image makes no sense.

Actually, all light rays obey the Law of Reflection, which is easily seen on smooth surfaces. This law states that when light hits a surface at an angle (the incidence angle), and reflects at another angle (the reflection angle), the two angles are equal. This means when light is incident on a smooth surface, it follows a precise path, one that is symmetrical

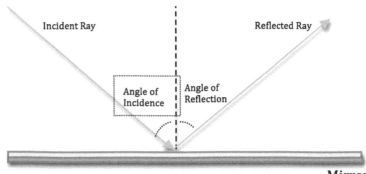

and can be predicted. In this chapter, you'll experience and understand these facts with some fun and simple activities.

One useful application of mirrors is that of a periscope, a device that allows the user to view objects while he or she remains hidden. A simple periscope consists of a long tube and mirrors placed at each end. Light from the object enters from one end, reflects from one mirror to the other, and exits from the eyepiece to the observer.

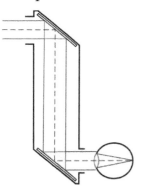

ACTIVITIES

We will explore the Law of Reflection by tracing the light incident on a mirror. Then we will build a periscope, watch how light travels from one end to the other, and observe objects placed on one end through the eyepiece.

REFLECTION ANGLE

Need: mirror, flashlight, aluminum foil, exacto knife, protractor, sheet

Procedure:

1. Place a mirror along the horizontal line of a protractor (shown here).

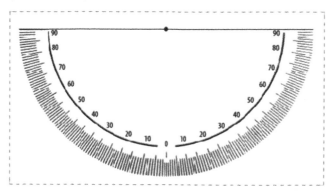

2. Cover the flashlight with a piece of aluminum foil and cut a vertical slit to let a thin beam through.

3. Place flashlight on the sheet facing the mirror at an angle.

4. Direct the light beam toward the mirror and aim for the mirror's center point.

5. Trace the incident and reflected beams.

6. Repeat for three different angles and record results in table provided here. They should be close.

Incident angle			
Reflected angle			

PERISCOPES

Need: 2 mirrors, an empty tissue or shoe box, flashlight with aluminum foil, exacto knife

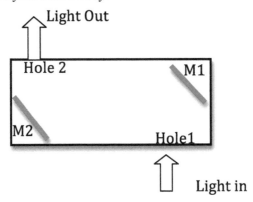

1. Remove the top side of the box, then cut two holes: a 1-inch square hole to let light in; another square, this one 2 inches square, to allow light to exit the box.

2. Place each mirror opposite the holes at an angle, to be determined in steps 3 through 6.

3. Shine the flashlight beam through the aluminum foil straight to the first mirror (M1) from the "light in" hole.

4. Tweak the position of M1 so that the beam reaches mirror 2 (M2).

5. Now tweak M2 so that the beam reflected goes out straight (the "light out" hole).

6. Trace the light beam as it travels in the diagram to the right.

7. Once the alignment is done, you should be able to see objects placed at the second hole while looking through hole #1.

REVERSE REFLECTONS

1. Write a word or short message on a small piece of paper.

2. Place it in front of either Mirror 1 or 2. What do you see? _____

3. Place the message by hole #2, and look through hole 1. What do you see?

Each mirror is reversing the reflection once. So, if you let it reflect through the two mirrors of the periscope, you can read it easily.

GOD'S LIGHT

During previous lessons, we mentioned Jesus as the light of the world, who shines His light on us so we can know Him. If you are someone who has trusted that light, you will walk with Him, talk to Him, and listen to Him. He will no longer be a mystery to you, nor will you have to hide and stay in darkness, ashamed of your sins.

1. Read **2 Corinthians 3:16-18** (*NLT*), where the apostle Paul describes how a Christian is changed.

   But whenever anyone turns to the Lord, the veil is taken away. Now the Lord is the Spirit, and where the Spirit of the Lord is, there is freedom. And we all, who with unveiled faces contemplate the Lord's glory, are being transformed into his image with ever-increasing glory, which comes from the Lord, who is the Spirit.

   - Paul says that whenever someone turns to the Lord, he or she is (note: more than one answer may be correct):

     a. embarrassed

     b. able to see clearly

     c. freed by His Spirit

   - Our transformation into His image occurs:

     a. through the Spirit of the Lord

     b. continuously

     c. through us alone

   - Those whose faith is in Christ, we:

     a. deny it

     b. keep quiet

     c. reflect it to others

A person who turns to Christ is free to enjoy God's glory and is unafraid to get closer to Him. He feels safe and free to reveal the truth that he knows to others. He becomes like a mirror of God, reflecting His light to others. Also, it is the Spirit of the Lord, the Holy Spirit, who brings us to Him and changes us as we walk more closely with Him.

2. Read **Acts 1:3-5, 8** (*NLT*) to learn more about the Holy Spirit.

During the forty days after he suffered and died, he appeared to the apostles from time to time, and he proved to them in many ways that he was actually alive. And he talked to them about the Kingdom of God. Once when he was eating with them, he commanded them, "Do not leave Jerusalem until the Father sends you the gift he promised, as I told you before. John baptized with water, but in just a few days you will be baptized with the Holy Spirit.

"But you will receive power when the Holy Spirit comes upon you. And you will be my witnesses, telling people about me everywhere—in Jerusalem, throughout Judea, in Samaria, and to the ends of the earth."

- Jesus appeared to the apostles so He could (more than one answer may be correct):

  a. prove to them He was alive

  b. talk to them about the kingdom of God

- What is the gift the Father promised He would send?

  a. John

  b. the Holy Spirit

  c. Jerusalem

Later Jesus ascended to heaven and the disciples remained together in prayer.

In Acts 2, on the day of Pentecost, the Father sent the Holy Spirit to the disciples, giving them all the special power of speaking many languages. So they went out and spoke to Jews, who lived in many other countries and spoke in different languages, but had come to Jerusalem on that day to celebrate the Pentecost festival.

3. Read **Acts 2:6-8, 12, 13** to see how the people reacted.

When they heard this sound, a crowd came together in bewilderment, because each one heard their own language being spoken. Utterly amazed, they asked: "Aren't all these who are speaking Galileans? Then how is it that each of us hears them in our native language?"

Amazed and perplexed. "What can this mean?" they asked one another. Some, however, made fun of them and said, "They have had too much wine."

- The Jews of different nationalities who heard the disciples speak were:

a. amazed

b. not bothered

c. mocking them (some of them)

Then Peter stood up and explained the reason these men had the power of speaking in their languages. First, he told them that the Great God, who loved Israel, had promised the Messiah through the prophets. Then he said the Messiah was Jesus, who had been crucified earlier that year, rose from the dead on the third day, and had ascended to His Father in Heaven. Finally, Peter said that God sent the Holy Spirit to dwell with all those who repent and are baptized in the name of Jesus Christ.

4. Read **Acts 2:41** to learn about the result of this outpouring of the Holy Spirit.

*Those who believed what Peter said were baptized and added to the church that day—about three thousand in all.(**NLT**)*

Very likely, some of those who responded to the Gospel message returned to their homelands with this great news. This tells us God wants the whole world to know the Gospel message!

Today, the Holy Spirit empowers some Christians to become missionaries to different parts of the world, others to work in local communities—such as with the homeless, in schools, and on college campuses—and many to witness to their neighbors and families. Wherever God calls the believers in Christ to go, they will do so with the help of the Holy Spirit.

REFLECTION

- Spend time reflecting on the power of the Holy Spirit given to the disciples.

- If you have accepted Jesus into your heart, pray about getting baptized.

MEMORY VERSE: ACTS 2:38

Peter replied, "Repent and be baptized, every one of you, in the name of Jesus Christ for the forgiveness of your sins. And you will receive the gift of the Holy Spirit."

CHAPTER SEVEN

WHICH IS THE RIGHT PATH?

INTRODUCTION

By this time, you may be getting increasingly curious about light, and asking more questions. One question that fishermen probably asked thousands of years ago was regarding the location of fish in the water. Over time they learned that fish always appear closer than they actually are, and so they began to aim deeper with their spears to hit their target.

In this lesson, we're going to explore in greater detail what happens to light in a transparent substance. We'll also learn how to be Bible scholars and explore Psalm 119, which teaches us about the importance of knowing God's Word.

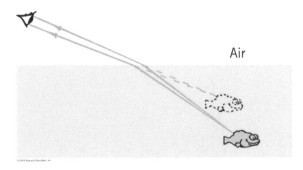

Air

BACKGROUND

We've already learned that when traveling light encounters a transparent substance, it goes through. What also happens is shown in the figure, where you can see that light bends as it travels from air into water. This happens because water is denser than air, and therefore light slows down. Here's another way to think of it: consider how slow you walk in a swimming pool compared to walking in air!

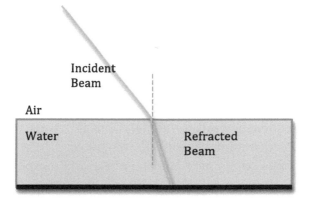

When light bends after entering another transparent material, we say that it *refracts*. Actually, the Law of Refraction allows one to precisely calculate how much the light will bend. This law is also called Snell's Law as it is named after scientist Willebrord Snellius (1580-1627). Snellius spent many years studying the works of other scientists, and he experimented until he developed the Law of Refraction. This law is the basis of the lens technology used in the production of eyeglasses, cameras, and telescopes.

Some of you may ask this question: What happens when light moves from water to air instead of from air to water? In this case, since air is less dense than water, light will speed up and refract at a larger angle. A small portion will be reflected back in the water.

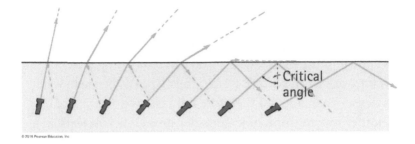

Critical angle

© 2015 Pearson Education, Inc.

In the figure shown here, you see light shining from the flashlight in water at increasing angles from left to right. Light also gets refracted at larger angles until it reaches the boundary and starts to bend inward! It is now totally reflected inside the water!

This fabulous scientific reality, called *total internal reflection*, provides the basis for fiber-optic cables, which transmit information and images through long cables. These are used by telephone companies, computer networks, hospital surgeries, and beautiful light displays.

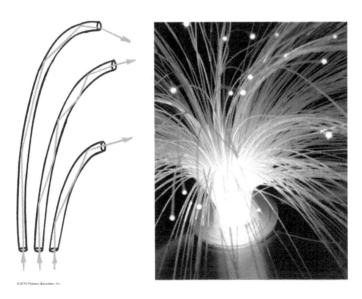

© 2015 Pearson Education, Inc.

ACTIVITIES

We will perform just a few of the fun activities a person can do with refraction. They all look like magic! Try to perform them for your family and friends!

DID THE STRAW BEND?

Need: A clear jar, water, a straw, a ruler

1. Rest the straw diagonally in an empty glass and draw what you see.

2. Now fill the glass halfway with water. Does the straw appear thicker in water? _____

3. Align a ruler with the part of the straw outside the water. Is the ruler aligned with the part of straw inside the water? _____

Does the straw look straight or bent? _____

Add what you observe to the drawing,

4. Hold the straw vertically.

Does the straw appear bent? _____

Does the straw appear thicker? _____

The object looks straight when the straw is:

a. vertical   or   **b.** horizontal

WHERE IS THE COIN?

Need: an _opaque_ bowl or cup, a coin, tape, a pitcher of water, one helper

1. Tape a coin firmly at the bottom (inside) of the bowl.

2. Sit or stand around the bowl so that the coin is seen.

3. Move back until the last of the coin is seen. *Do not move until the next step.*

4. Your helper will fill the bowl with water slowly, about 1 inch at a time.

5. During this process, the observer should see the coin "pop up" without it having moved at all.

TOTAL INTERNAL REFLECTION!

***Need:** a glass jar filled with water, a pencil, one helper*

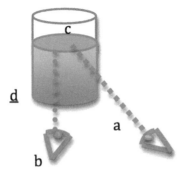

Hold a pencil over the water at position **c.**

Look toward the top of the water from various angles between the two positions **a** and **b.**

You should be able to see the pen from position **b**, but not **a**. In fact, the surface should look like a mirror because it reflects light internally for angles as wide as a. If you lower the pencil, it will seem like it is piercing through a mirror!

Place the glass on the edge of a table, and lay the pencil at position **d.** Look through the water from position **a.** You should be able to see the image of the pencil due to total internal reflection.

GOD'S LIGHT

Through his careful studies, Snellius provided the world with the refraction law, which explained many things that were not clear to the eye. This resulted in many useful discoveries that were helpful for mankind.

In the same way, studying God's Word teaches about His character and how He wants us to live.

1. An excellent passage that explains the importance of knowing God's Word is Psalm 119. Find it in your Bible.

- Do you notice that it is divided into many sections? The titles of these sections are the alphabet of the Hebrew language. Count and write the number of sections: _____

- Now go to the end of Psalm 119 and find and write the total number of its verses: _____

James Maxwell, the scientist we learned about in chapter two, could recite the entire Psalm 119 at the age of eight, all one hundred and seventy-six verses![1]

2. Look through this Psalm, read the verses below from your Bible, and fill in the blanks.

Psalm 119:2 – *Those who walk according to the **law** of the Lord are* _____.

Psalm 119:15 – *They* _____ *on God's **precepts**.*

Psalm 119:24 – *God's **statutes** are their* _____.

Psalm 119:32 – *They* _____ *in the paths of His **commands**.*

Psalm 119:83 – *They do* _____ _____ *the Lord's **decrees**.*

Psalm 119:169 – *The **Word** gives us* _____.

Throughout Psalm 119, the author is pointing to the importance of staying close to God's law, which also means His precepts, statutes, commands, decrees, and Word. The psalmist shows that following God's law has numerous blessings. He emphasizes the importance of meditating on God's precepts, delighting in them, following them with all of our heart, and not forgetting them. This way we have understanding and are less likely to stumble.

3. This same idea is repeated in other psalms in addition to 119. For example, King David says in Psalm 19:8:

> *The precepts of the LORD are right,*
> *giving joy to the heart.*
>
> *The commands of the LORD are radiant,*
> *giving light to the eyes.*

- How are the precepts of the Lord? _____
  And what do they cause? _____

- What do the commands of the Lord give?
  _____

King David authored seventy-three other psalms, which were honest revelations of his heart, whether he was happy or sad, peaceful or anguished. No wonder he is known as the man after God's own heart! David was also inspired by the Holy Spirit to prophecy many times about the Messiah, who would be his descendant. He described who He was and the details about his life, death, and resurrection!

4. Read prophecies of King David about Jesus, and look up the verses on the right.

King David's Prophecy Verse	Fulfillment
Psalm 2:7 – *I will proclaim the LORD's decree: He said to me, "You are my son; today I have become your father."*	**Hebrews 1:5, 6**
Psalm 22:1 – *My God, my God, why have you forsaken me?*	**Matthew 27:46**
Psalm 22:18 – *They divide my clothes among them and cast lots for my garment.*	**Matthew 27:35, John 19:23, 24**
Psalm 16:10 – *Because you will not abandon me to the realm of the dead, nor will you let your faithful one see decay.*	**Luke 24:5, 6**

- Write your comments on what you think of these prophecies about Jesus:

_____

_____

_____

While Psalm 119 encourages us to know God's commands, the psalms of David invite us to know God personally and prepare us for the coming of his Son, Jesus. They prepare us for God's plan. God the Father sent his only Son to die in our place and conquer death.

5. Read **John 14:6, 7**, when Jesus answered his disciple Thomas on how he could know the way to the Father.

"I am the way and the truth and the life. No one comes to the Father except through me. If you really

63

knew me, you know my Father as well. From now on, you do know him and have seen him."

- Who does Jesus lead us to?

  _____

- Is there another way?

  _____

As the *way*, Jesus is the path to the Father. As the *truth*, He is the reality of all God's promises. As the *life*, He joins His divine life to us, both now and eternally.

REFLECTIONS

- Do you understand the importance of reading God's Word? _____
- Can you describe how Jesus is the way for you?

  _____

MEMORY VERSES: PSALM 119:105, JOHN 14:6

Your word is a lamp for my feet, a light on my path.

"I am the way and the truth and the life. No one comes to the Father except through me."

CHAPTER EIGHT

FOCUS ON THE LIGHT!

INTRODUCTION

During your yearly doctor's exam, your eyesight is usually checked by reading from a chart 20 feet away. If you are able to read the fourth line from the bottom, your vision is a very healthy "20/20"! If not, you will be advised to see an optometrist, who can prescribe you glasses. In this lesson we will learn how your eyes see and how glasses can correct vision problems. Then we will learn about the apostle Paul, who encountered Jesus while Paul was on his way to persecute Jesus' followers.

E	1	20/200
F P	2	20/100
T O Z	3	20/70
L P E D	4	20/50
P E C F D	5	20/40
E D F C Z P	6	20/30
F E L O P Z D	7	20/25
D E F P O T E C	8	20/20
L E F O D P C T	9	
F D P L T C E O	10	
P E F O L C F T D	11	

BACKGROUND

Our eye is an amazing instrument made of various transparent substances all trapped in a one-inch ball! Light first enters the eye from the cornea and bends, traveling to the lens, which has a convex shape. The lens bends the light from the observed object one more time to form an image by the fovea on the retina. The optic nerves pick up the light signals and send them to the brain. The image of the object is flipped upside down, but the brain flips it back so it seems upright to us!

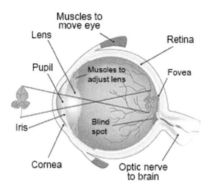

The focus of the lens depends on its curvature. For example, lenses A, B, and C show three convex lenses with different curvatures. Lens A is the most curved and has the closest focus. The less curved the lens, the longer the focus. The lens in our eye is sustained by muscles that help adjust its focus.

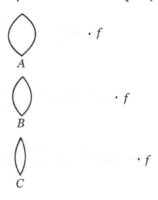

In a normal eye, the cornea and lens focus the image on the retina, forming a clear image. This is not always the case, though, and many people need their vision corrected.

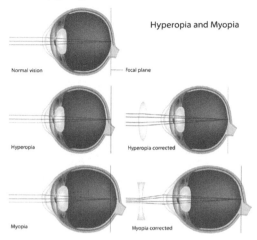

Hyperopia and Myopia

Normal vision — Focal plane

Hyperopia — Hyperopia corrected

Myopia — Myopia corrected

If an eye suffers from *hyperopia*, the focus is beyond the retina and the image is therefore blurry. A convex lens is used to gather the light rays so the eye can focus sooner to form a clear image on the retina. If an eye suffers from *myopia*, its focus is before the retina, and the image is, again, blurry. A concave lens is used to spread the light rays and shifts the eye's focus further to form a clear image on the retina.

An optometrist gives an eyeglass or lens prescription using a machine called a refractor, which conveniently switches the lenses with different focusing abilities. The patients look through the eyepieces while the doctor asks how clearly they are seeing.

Laser surgeries are also successful procedures that reshape the cornea so the images focus on the retina. They offer permanent solutions and freedom from eyeglass and lens prescriptions for those who qualify.

ACTIVITIES WITH LENSES

The following activities will help you explore the effect of curvature of a lens on the focus.

FOCUS

Need: Different sizes of glass jars filled with water, a shoe box painted black on the inside, flashlight or sunlight, index card

1. Cut a square 2" x 2" hole in the bottom center of a narrow side of the shoe box.

2. Cut two vertical slits (1" high x 1/8" wide, and 1/4" apart) on the bottom center of an index card side.

3. Put the light source outside the box, letting light through the slits. Observe the two light beams that pass through.

4. Place the jar in the box at a point where it blocks the light beams.

5. Observe the outcome: Do the light beams focus?

_____

6. Try this with different sizes of jars and observe what happens.

   The wider jars have a focus that is:

   a. closer   or   **b.** farther?

68

IMAGES WITH LENSES

Need: *magnifying glass, a screen (or white wall), daylight*

1. Stand where you can see a scenery far away.

2. Hold the lens between the scenery and the screen (or wall).

3. Adjust the lens until you clearly see the image of the scenery on the screen.

The image should be inverted.

TEST MYOPIC AND HYPEROPIC GLASSES

Need: *black pocket comb, one pair of eyeglasses with strong prescription for a myopic/shortsighted person(6 and over), flashlight*

1. Shine light through the comb, enabling you to see thin line beams.

2. Intercept with one lens of glasses .

3. Watch the beams spread. The stronger the prescription, the more the beams spread.

GOD'S LIGHT

After learning about vision, let's meet Saul, a Jewish rabbi whose sole focus was to arrest Christians to stop them from spreading the news about Christ. He was the one who oversaw the death of Stephen when they stoned him (Acts 7:59).

1. Read **Acts 8:1-3** to learn more.

On that day a great persecution broke out against the church in Jerusalem, and all except the apostles were scattered throughout Judea and Samaria. Godly men buried Stephen and mourned deeply for him. But Saul began to destroy the church. Going from house to house, he dragged off both men and women and put them in prison.

- What happened to the church members?

  _____

- Who stayed in Jerusalem?

  _____

- What was Saul focused on doing?

  _____

Saul even set out on a long journey to the foreign city of Damascus so he could capture the Christians there. On his way there, he encountered Jesus! The story is found in **Acts 9:1-22**.

2. Read **Acts 9:3-6**.

As he neared Damascus on his journey, suddenly a light from heaven flashed around him. He fell to the ground and heard a voice say to him, "Saul, Saul, why do you persecute me?"

"Who are you, Lord?" Saul asked.

"I am Jesus, whom you are persecuting," he replied. "Now get up and go into the city, and you will be told what you must do."

- Who did Jesus say Saul was persecuting?

_____

- Why didn't Jesus simply say: "Why are you persecuting the Christians?"

_____

- Did you notice this? Saul calls Jesus: L_____!

Jesus' followers are Christ's body on earth! Attacking any Christian hurts the whole body. Yet Paul called the One he had been persecuting "Lord." In fact, from this day on, Saul follows Jesus' orders!

The next three days, Saul remained blind and fasted from food and drink. He had a vision that a man named Ananias would heal him. Ananias, a follower of Christ living in Damascus, also heard from the Lord—but his calling was to go visit Saul and restore his vision! He was afraid because he had heard of Saul's wrath towards Christians.

3. Read **Acts 9:15, 16.**

But the Lord said to Ananias, "Go! This man is my chosen instrument to proclaim my name to the Gentiles and their kings and to the people of Israel.

I will show him how much he must suffer for my name."

- Can God choose anyone to be his follower?

_____

- What is this act of God about?

a. His grace

b. His need to seek revenge

c. His reward for what Saul did

Ananias obeyed the Lord and went to meet Saul, healing him from his blindness. Saul got baptized, regained his strength, and spent time with the disciples of Jesus before beginning his ministry.

4. Read **Acts 9:20-22.**

At once he began to preach in the synagogues that Jesus is the Son of God. All those who heard him were astonished and asked, "Isn't he the man who raised havoc in Jerusalem among those who call on this name? And hasn't he come here to take them as prisoners to the chief priests?" Yet Saul grew more and more powerful and baffled the Jews living in Damascus by proving that Jesus is the Messiah.

What an amazing transformation! At first, Saul was very zealous for his Jewish beliefs and even persecuted Christians. After he became a Christian, Saul was the one to escape because the Jews wanted to kill him! Meanwhile, the church grew and spread even more, with much of that growth due to his heroic acts.

Jesus first blinded Saul as if to show him he was living in spiritual darkness. But when Saul was healed from his blindness, his focus switched to Christ, whom he obeyed and served the rest of his life. A short time later, his name was changed to Paul. Paul started several churches and wrote many letters to teach believers in Jesus. These are still in the Bible and have helped Christians throughout all generations.

5. Read from one of his letters to Christians in the city of Philippi (**Philippians 3:13, 14**).

But one thing I do: Forgetting what is behind and straining toward what is ahead, I press on toward the goal to win the prize for which God has called me heavenward in Christ Jesus.

- What things does Paul forget?

  _____

- What does he concentrate on?

  _____

WHERE IS YOUR FOCUS?

- What are your goals at this point in your life?

  _____

  _____

  _____

- Do you involve Jesus in your goals? _____
- Do your past mistakes still bother you? _____
  If yes, ask Jesus to forgive you.
- Pray for yourself or someone who needs the grace of Jesus.

MEMORY VERSE: PHILIPPIANS 3:14

I press on toward the goal to win the prize for which God has called me heavenward in Christ Jesus.

CHAPTER NINE

IS THIS LIGHT YOUR HOPE?

INTRODUCTION

Remember the last time you saw a rainbow in the sky? It is such a marvelous sight that one has to share what they've seen with everyone around them! It brings great joy to the heart! In this lesson, we will explore the formation of rainbows and create some of our own as well. Then we will visit the time in the Bible when God made a covenant with Noah by revealing the rainbow, giving much hope to the generations after him. We will also learn about God's covenants with Abraham, Moses, King David, and all mankind.

9.4,5

BACKGROUND

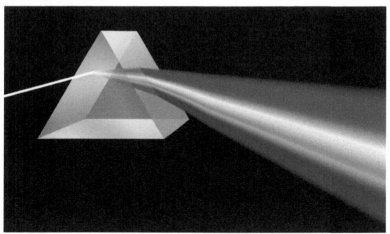

The light from the sun and other light sources appear white to us. Actually, this light consists of a group of colors that look white when combined. If a beam of white light goes through a transparent object that is angled or round, it splits into the colored beams of a rainbow. (You have likely heard of the first letters of the colors forming: ROYGBIV.) This is shown clearly by a prism.

A rainbow is formed in the sky when sunlight passes through millions of water droplets, which act like a prism. We usually see a rainbow after a storm, as we stand looking

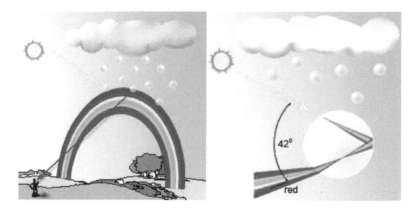

at the clouds with the sun behind us shining on the clouds. Sunlight refracts inside each water droplet and splits into various colors. Then each color wave reflects at the other end

and refracts outward again. Our eyes see all the rays that reach them. Rainbows also can be seen when sunlight is shining from behind us onto water fountains, or when it goes through a glass of water or crystal object.

The ROYGBIV color pattern is produced in other ways as well. For example, a rainbow pattern appears on the reflective surface of a CD under a light beam. With the help of a microscope, a close look at a CD reveals a plastic cover over aluminum and tiny ridges responsible for splitting the light into different colors. Rainbow patterns also appear on soap bubbles and puddles of oil because the thickness on their surface changes, so the different colors split.

ACTIVITIES

Learn ways to split light from the sun and other light sources into a rainbow.

SPLIT LIGHT USING A PRISM

Split light using a prism with sunlight or flashlight

Need: Prism, sunlight, white paper

1. Let sunlight shine on the prism from one side.
2. Place the white paper on the other side.
3. Adjust the prism until you see the rainbow spectrum on the paper.

On a cloudy day or nighttime, you will need a strong flashlight (not LED), white screen, index card, scissors

1. Make a slit 1/8-inch wide and 1-inch long on the index card.
2. Direct the flashlight through the slit and let it go through the prism.
3. Tweak the prism until you see a rainbow spot on the screen.

SPLIT LIGHT USING A MIRROR AND WATER
Split light using a mirror and water with sunlight or flashlight

Need: *Mirror, water, 9" x 12" shallow pan, white paper*

1. Fill two-thirds of the pan with water.

2. Hold mirror inside the water, at an angle, toward the sun.

3. Hold the white sheet opposite the mirror, careful not to block the sunlight.

4. Slowly change the mirror angle until you see the rainbow spectrum on the paper. (The mirror and water together act like a prism)

On a cloudy day or nighttime, you will need a *strong flashlight (not LED), Aluminum foil, scissors.*

1. Cut a piece of Aluminum foil big enough to cover the beam from the flashlight

2. Make a thin 1-inch slit in the center of foil. A nice beam should form. Repeat the same procedure as with the sun.

MORE RAINBOWS

- On a sunny day, blow bubbles or hold a hose spraying water at an angle, standing with your back toward the sun.

- Reflect a light beam from your flashlight with a CD or DVD. You'll get rainbow beams on the wall.

GOD'S LIGHT

Do you remember the story of the great flood? The story is told in Genesis chapters 6-9, when God asked a righteous man, Noah, to build an arc so his family and pairs of all animals would be spared from a worldwide flood. The rest of mankind (and animals) perished, because men and women had turned wicked in God's eyes. Yet after the flood, by placing a rainbow, He made his first covenant with Noah, and all generations thereafter, to give them hope.

1. Read **Genesis 9:12-15** to understand why (emphasis is mine).

And God said, "This is the sign of the <u>covenant</u> I am making between me and you and every living creature with you, a <u>covenant</u> for all generations to come: I have set my <u>rainbow</u> in the clouds, and it will be the sign of the <u>covenant</u> between me and the earth. Whenever I bring clouds over the earth and the <u>rainbow</u> appears in the clouds, I will remember my <u>covenant</u> between me and you and all living creatures of every kind. Never again will the waters become a flood to destroy all life.

So God made the **first covenant** with _____.
The covenant stated that He would not _____ all life. This gave **Noah** and his family _____.
God made **more covenants** with mankind through other prophets.

2. Read **Genesis 17:1-4** to find out about God's covenant with Abraham, who was a godly man married to Sarah. The two were old in age, and did not have any children.

When Abram was ninety-nine years old, the LORD appeared to him and said, "I am God Almighty; walk before me faithfully

*and be blameless. Then I will make my covenant between
me and you and will greatly increase your numbers."*

*Abram fell facedown, and God said to him, "As for me, this is
my <u>covenant</u> with you: You will be the father of many nations."*

- God made a **covenant** with _____,
  stating that He would make him the father of many

  _____.

- This gave him _____ because it promised him _____.

3. Read **Exodus 34:28** and **34:11** to learn about the covenant God made with Moses, whom He had chosen to
   lead the Israelites out of Egypt.

   *Moses was there with the Lord forty days and forty
   nights without eating bread or drinking water. And
   he wrote on the tablets the words of the covenant—
   the Ten Commandments (Exodus 34:28).*

   *Obey what I command you today. I will drive out
   before you the Amorites, Canaanites, Hittites,
   Perizzites, Hivites and Jebusites (Exodus 34:11).*

- God made a **covenant** with **Moses:** *If the people followed the* _____ _____ , *God
  would* _____ *them. This gave them*

  _____.

God also gave Moses many more laws that required sacrific-
ing an animal whenever the Israelites committed a sin.

4. Read **Leviticus 4:32-35** to see what they had to do
   (emphasis is mine).

But if he brings a lamb as his offering for a sin offering, he shall bring it, a female without defect. He shall lay his hand on the head of the sin offering and slay it for a sin offering in the place where they slay the burnt offering. The priest is to take some of the blood of the sin offering with his finger and put it on the horns of the altar of burnt offering, and all the rest of its blood he shall pour out at the base of the altar. Then he shall remove all its fat, just as the fat of the lamb is removed from the sacrifice of the peace offerings, and the priest shall offer them up in smoke on the altar, on the offerings by fire to the LORD. Thus the priest shall make **atonement** *for him in regard to his sin which he has committed, and he will be* **forgiven.**

- If they sinned, they had to sacrifice a lamb without _____ by shedding its _____. It was then that God _____ them and they had _____ again.

Since men sin often, they probably had to perform this sacrifice regularly. Imagine all the work involved to keep up with the details!

5. Read **Luke 22:19, 20** to remember Jesus words during his last supper with the disciples

And he took bread, gave thanks and broke it, and gave it to them, saying, "This is my body given for you; do this in remembrance of me."

In the same way, after the supper he took the cup, saying, "This cup is the new covenant in my blood, which is poured out for you."

- The **new Covenant** with God was to all mankind through _____. The bread during communion represents his _____ given for you. The wine in the cup represents his _____ that was shed so that _____ sins would be forgiven.

- Jesus died for **our** _____ as a sin offering to be the _____ that will cleanse us.

- Just like the **Rainbow** gave _____ to Noah's family, **Jesus** gives you and me _____ for eternity.

REFLECTIONS

- How does Jesus offer you hope?

  _____

- Does your faith in him strengthen you in every good deed and word?

  _____

Memory Verse: 2 Thessalonians 2:16, 17

May our Lord Jesus Christ himself and God our Father, who loved us and by his grace gave us eternal encouragement and good hope, encourage your hearts and strengthen you in every good deed and word.

CHAPTER TEN

ARE YOU IN HIS LIGHT?

INTRODUCTION

In addition to creating light to be the source of life on earth, our great God also offered it to us as a source of enjoyment. Consider the beautiful sceneries of the rainbow, auroras, and sunsets. In this lesson, we will continue learning about Newton's discoveries with colors, and we will examine the wave nature of light. We will appreciate the different gifts God has blessed us with, and learn how to use them for His glory.

BACKGROUND

Some of the many contributions to science Sir Isaac Newton made in the seventeenth century included his discoveries in the field of color and light. Until then, it was believed that prisms simply created colors. Newton performed experiments to show the reason colored beams come from a prism.

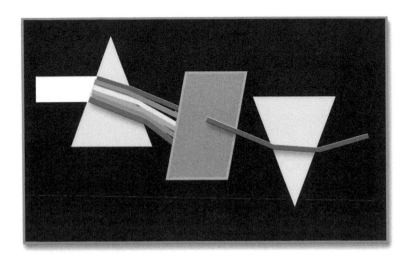

First, he used a prism to split white light from the sun into rainbow color beams. He then captured the red color and passed it through another prism, and the light came out red again. This showed that the prism didn't create rainbow beams from a single color.

In another experiment, Newton directed all the colored beams exiting one prism to another prism, this one inverted, and the outcome was white light. So he reached the conclusion that white light is a mixture of all the colors that split upon entering the prism.

When white light enters a prism, the different colors are separated because they travel at different speeds and no longer overlap. The waves of red light are spread out the

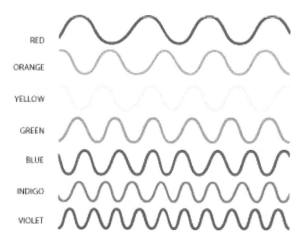

RED
ORANGE
YELLOW
GREEN
BLUE
INDIGO
VIOLET

most, and these bend the least when they enter the prism. The waves of violet light are more dense, and they bend the most when they enter the prism. When all these light beams overlap, their combined energy looks white.

Newton also invented the color wheel, which he painted with the familiar acronym ROYGBIV. When spun fast, the color wheel appears white. Once more, this indicates that white light is a combination of the ROYGBIV colors. Since the eye is no longer able to distinguish the colors separately because they are moving so fast, it perceives the whole group together as white.

ACTIVITY: COLOR WHEEL TO COMBINE ROYGBIV

Goal: make rainbow color wheels and spin them fast using a whirligig, a mini-engine, or a top. We are using only six colors and leaving indigo out since it is hard to find a good shade. This shouldn't affect the results.

Need: Heavy cardboard, paper, compass, 6 coloring pencils (Red, Orange, Yellow, Green, Blue, Violet), sharpened pencil, scissors, glue stick, 24-inch-long twined string

1. Trace and cut two 3-inch circles on paper and one from a cardboard.

2. Sketch twelve sections on the paper discs.

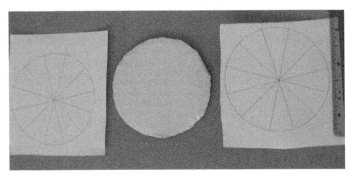

3. Color both paper circles with all **ROYGBV** colors on alternate sections. (Color exact proportions on one side, but add more of one color on the other side.)

4. Glue the colored discs on the cardboard bases.

5. Use a sharp pencil to pierce 3/8-inch holes, one-half inch apart. Slip the two ends of the 24-inch string from the holes and tie it.

6. Pull the string from both sides of the disc in the center, and slip your index fingers on each end.

7. Spin the disc by making fast circular motions (about 30 times) until the string twirls, then immediately change the motion of your hands toward and away from the disc. The disc should now be twirling. This could take a few tries.

8. Notice the perceived wheel color while twirling fast: *The disc side with equal* **ROYGBV** *color proportions should appear white, but the side with more of one color will be less white.*

ALTERNATE OPTION WITH MINI-ENGINE FOR STEPS 4-7:

Need: same supplies as previous setup except for 24-inch string, a DC-powered mini-motor (1.5-3V), mounted batteries, and 2 alligator clip wires

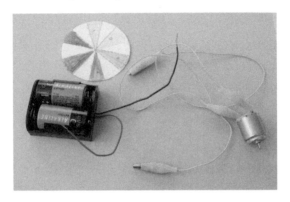

Repeat steps 1 – 4 as with the previous experiment.

5. Pierce one hole in the center of the disc.

6. Mount disc on the mini-engine.

7. Use alligators to connect engine to the battery wires.

8. The wheel will spin fast and blend all colors to white on the side with equal **ROYGBV** proportions.

GOD'S LIGHT

Just as the rainbow colors with different energies combine to give white light, people with different skills and gifts often unite for a common purpose. On a sports team, for example, it's important that each player does his or her part for the team to play well. In a factory, each worker has a different task, but all must be completed to obtain a good product.

In the same way, Christians gather in a church to worship and serve the Lord with their unique talents and gifts. The apostles Paul and Peter wrote on this very subject with the goal of keeping the churches united.

1. Read **1 Corinthians 12:4-6, 11.**

There are different kinds of gifts, but the same Spirit distributes them. There are different kinds of service, but the same Lord. There are different kinds of working, but in all of them and in everyone it is the same God at work.

All these are the work of one and the same Spirit, and he distributes them to each one, just as he determines.

- No matter what gift a person is given, each gift is given by the same _____.
- Who determines these gifts?

  _____

- Name ways to serve in the church

  _____

  _____

In the rest of 1 Corinthians, Paul talks about the importance of all the jobs in a church, just as each part of our body is important. For example, we need our eyes, ears, nose, feet, hands, and all other body parts to fully function. If any part is hurting, our whole body is affected. In the same way, if someone at church is hurting or not doing their part well, the whole church body is affected and concerned. It is important that the rest of the body pray about the situation so they will be shown what they can do.

2. Read **Acts 6:3-6** to learn how the apostles chose seven men who helped them distribute food so they could have time to teach.

"Brothers and sisters, choose seven men from among you who are known to be full of the Spirit and wisdom. We will turn this responsibility over to them and will give our attention to prayer and the ministry of the word." This proposal pleased the whole group. They chose Stephen, a man full of faith and of the Holy Spirit; also Philip, Procorus, Nicanor, Timon, Parmenas, and Nicolas from Antioch, a convert to Judaism. They presented these men to the apostles, who prayed and laid their hands on them.

• What qualities marked the seven chosen helpers?

  _____

  _____

• What did the apostles do when these men were presented to them?

  _____

  _____

• Therefore, since everyone shared the jobs with prayer and unity in the Spirit, the Word of God spread rapidly and the number of Christians increased. God's light shines more powerfully when everyone working for him does their part eagerly and prayerfully.

3. Read **1 Peter 4:8-11** to learn more about how one should serve in a church.

Above all, love each other deeply, because love covers over a multitude of sins. Offer hospitality to one another without grumbling. Each of you should use whatever gift you have received to serve others, as faithful stewards of God's grace in its various forms. If anyone speaks, they should do so as one who speaks the very words of God. If anyone serves, they should do so with the strength God provides, so that in all things God may be praised through Jesus Christ. To him be the glory and the power for ever and ever. Amen.

- Why should we love each other?

  _____

- How should we offer hospitality to one another?

  _____

- Whom should we serve?

  _____

- Whose stewards are we?

  _____

- How should we speak?

  _____

- Whose strength should we rely on?

  _____

- Who should be glorified most and always?

  _____

It is clear from this passage that working lovingly with each other is very important at church and in other communities. In all we do, we must do it with God's help and remember to praise him always. It is only then that we are effective agents of His light to give hope to many who need to know that Jesus died for their sins so they can be part of His body.

HOW ABOUT YOU?
How would you like to serve in a church?

_____, _____

Will you make sure Jesus will always shine?

_____

Do you feel that you are in His light?

_____

Memory Verse: 1 Corinthians 12:4-6

There are different kinds of gifts, but the same Spirit distributes them. There are different kinds of service, but the same Lord. There are different kinds of working, but in all of them and in everyone it is the same God at work.

CHAPTER ELEVEN

WHAT IS THIS COLOR?

INTRODUCTION

God gave us the ability to distinguish close to 17 million different color shades! Scientists have explained this unique gift as they looked closely into the eye and understood the source of the different shades of color. In this lesson, we will explain how we perceive colors, and we will perform color addition with the primary colors of red, green, and blue. We'll then discuss Bible verses where eight different colors are used to tell us something about God's plan for us.

BACKGROUND

The retina in your eyes, located in the far back of the eye, contains two types of light-sensing cells: rods and cones. Rods help us see in the dark and sense motion, but not colors. Cones help us see colors and work best in bright light.

Photoreceptor cell

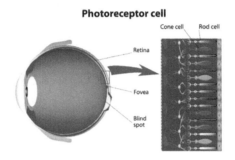

The cones in the eye are located in the *fovea*, and they contain chemicals that are sensitive to red (R), green (G), and blue (B) lights. When any light color with a given wavelength reaches the retina, the photocells sensitive to its energy will respond. They send electrical signals to the brain, which determines the color perceived depending on how much each of the R, G, and B pigments have been energized.

The red, green, and blue colors are considered the primary colors. When the RGB colors are added in pairs, they combine to produce the *secondary* colors of Magenta (= R+B), Yellow (=R+G), Cyan (=G+B). Where the three intersect, white color is perceived, the same as when the all rainbow colors blend. When people are color-blind, some of their RGB cones are malfunctioning, and they can only perceive a certain range of colors.

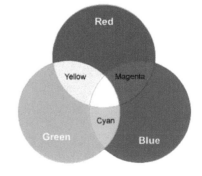

94

When the RGB colors are added in different proportions, they produce the millions of hues a normal eye is able to

perceive. For example, if Green is mixed with Magenta (= R+ B color), lighter shades of Magenta will be produced, depending on the proportion of Green added.

It was none other than James C. Maxwell, who we first met in chapter two, who expanded on the works of scientists Young and Forbes in developing a method that produces the different hues by combining primary and secondary colors. He tried these on a color wheel with various proportions of RGB colors and twirled them to test a new shade. In 1861, during his lectures on color theory at the Royal Institution in London, he led the shooting of the first color photograph! His findings formed the basis of colored pixels for the screens in TVs and computers!

ACTIVITIES

The activities below involve spinning color wheels with the primary RGB colors in pairs, and then with all three together. We'll also explore other interesting combinations.

COLOR ADDITION

Need: A 2" paper wheel, coloring pencils, spinning device (a mini-engine with battery; or whirligig)

- Color the paper wheels with the combinations listed in the table.

- Spin them and observe the color.

ROYGBIV	RBG	RG

RB	BG	YB

Rewrite the results in the form of equations.

$R + B + G =$ _____ . $R + O + Y + G + B + V =$ _____ .

Therefore, mixing the primary colors _____, _____, and _____ is enough for our eye to perceive white.

$G + B =$ _____ . $R + G =$ _____ . $R + B =$ _____ .
What color did you get when you mixed $Y + B$? _____
You should get a color close to white.

Remember that Y = _____ + _____.
So Y + B = _____ + _____ + B = _____!

In the same way, determine what color you would get if you mix:
C + R = _____ + _____ + R = _____, or
M + G = _____ + _____ + G = _____.

MORE WITH COLOR ADDITION
Expand on the previous activities by coloring a few wheels
with various proportions of primary and secondary colors,
just like James Maxwell might have done. For example, color
one with 1/2 R ; 1/8 G ; 3/8 R ; or 1/3 R , 1/3 G , 1/3 B.

EXPLORE YOUR COMPUTER'S COLOR PALETTE:
Explore your computer's color tool or an online color that
produce the different hues obtained from different combinations of R, G, B percentages. One of these websites is:
http://websitetips.com/colortools/colorblender/.

GOD'S LIGHT

Easter happens in springtime, when we are surrounded by colorful flowers, we color and decorate eggs, have Easter egg hunts, and eat jelly beans. Have you heard the Jelly Bean Prayer?[14] Its colorful message points to the story of Christ the King, who created us, suffered for us, died, and rose from the dead. It uses a set of colors to tell the meaning of Easter.

THE JELLY BEAN PRAYER

Red is for the blood He gave

Green is for the grass He made

is for the sun so bright

Orange is for the edge of night

Black is for the sins we made

White is for the grace He gave

Purple is for the hours of sorrow

Pink is for a new tomorrow.

Let's explore this poem by looking up Bible verses that refer to the significance of the colors. Discover the color that each verse is pointing to, and write it in the blank provided. The colors to choose from are: white, red, green, black, purple, yellow, orange, pink.

1 John 1:7 *But if we walk in the light, as he is in the light, we have fellowship with one another, and the blood of Jesus, his Son, purifies us from all sin.*

Psalm 23:2 *He makes me lie down in green pastures, he leads me beside quiet waters.*

_____

Job 37:21, 22 *Now no one can look at the sun, bright as it is in the skies after the wind has swept them clean. Out of the north he comes in golden splendor; God comes in awesome majesty.*

_____

Luke 23:44, 45 *It was now about noon, and darkness came over the whole land until three in the afternoon, for the sun stopped shining. And the curtain of the temple was torn in two.*

_____

Isaiah 9:2 *The people walking in darkness have seen a great light; on those living in the land of deep darkness a light has dawned.*

_____

Isaiah 1:18 *"Come now, and let us reason together," says the Lord. "Though your sins are like scarlet, they shall be as white as snow."*

_____

Mark 15:17 *And they clothed Him with purple; and they twisted a crown of thorns, [and] put it on His head* (**NLT**).

_____

Luke 24:1 *On the first day of the week, very early in the morning, the women took the spices they had prepared and went to the tomb.* _____

Next time you eat jelly beans, enjoy them with God in mind. Remember that He is the Creator of the world we live in, colorful and pleasing to the eye. is our eternal , who sent His only to die for us. Jesus gracefully endured a lot of pain and shed His pure blood for our **sins**. His **sacrifice,** followed by His resurrection, gives us hope for the days ahead, because we will be living with Him through eternity.

Some people refer to Easter as Resurrection Day, and it is the most important event in Christianity. Paul explains this in his first letter to the Corinthians, because a few people were saying there was no resurrection.

Read **1 Corinthians 15:3, 4.**

> *For what I received I passed on to you as of first importance: that Christ died for our sins according to the Scriptures, that he was buried, that he was raised on the third day according to the Scriptures.*

- Which three facts does Paul list as most important?

Christ _____, was _____, was _____

In verses 5-8, Paul describes how Jesus appeared to many after His resurrection, even to Paul! He explains how he did not deserve to meet Christ, because he had been His enemy and was persecuting His people.

Read **1 Corinthians 15:10.**

> *But by the grace of God I am what I am, and his grace to me was not without effect. No, I worked harder than all of them—yet not I, but the grace of God that was with me.*

- How did God's grace change Paul?

_____

Easter, therefore, is an opportunity to grow in admiration of God's saving grace for us, through His work on the cross and His resurrection. Let us be transformed by that grace, just like Paul, who relied on it to spread the Gospel to many parts of the world.

REFLECTIONS:

- Has Christ's resurrection changed you?

  _____

- Do you understand that His grace alone saves us?

  _____

- Are you ready to share this with someone else ?

Memory Verse: John 11:25

Jesus said to her, "I am the resurrection and the life. The one who believes in me will live, even though they die."

CHAPTER TWELVE

BE SALT AND LIGHT!

INTRODUCTION

After learning about light and its importance in our lives, it would be great to pass on what we know to others. We can do the same with our knowledge of who Jesus Christ is and what He has done for us. This is like being salt and light to others because we are helping preserve valuable information that will brighten generations to come. In this lesson, we will learn interesting facts about the history of salt, and we'll light a bulb connected to salty water in a circuit. Then we will discuss how a follower of Jesus Christ becomes salt and light to the world.

BACKGROUND

Salt has been a valuable mineral for thousands of years, and it used to be very difficult to extract. It was often called white gold because it was worth as much as gold. Many wars were fought over salt, or for pay to soldiers in salt, from the ancient Greeks until the American Civil War. (The word *salary* originated from the Latin word *salarium*, because soldiers were sometimes paid in salt.) Virtually every culture had customs relating to salt. People would share salt with their guests to show friendship and hospitality. Today, salt is cheap because many mines have been discovered under the earth, and plenty of the mineral can be extracted from seawater.

Salt is made of natural minerals, mainly sodium chloride (NaCl), which is a compound of sodium (Na) and chlorine (Cl) atoms arranged in cubic-formed crystals. Dry salt by itself is not useful until it is mixed with a liquid like water. When salt (or NaCl) dissolves in water (H_2O), the atoms Na (+) and Cl (-) break up and are attracted to the water molecules.

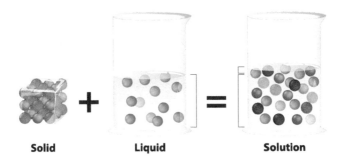

Solid   **Liquid**   **Solution**

Salt is an essential nutrient; our body needs about 1 teaspoon of it per day. On food labels, only sodium (Na) is listed because it is the part that matters when it comes to health. Na is released after salt dissolves with the liquids of our body. It keeps us hydrated, regulates our heartbeat, improves our brain function, helps with digestion, and heals wounds. Too much salt in a person's diet, however, can raise blood pressure, which is a leading cause of heart attack and stroke. Salt is also used in many industrial applications, such as preserving food, making bleach detergents, de-icing roads, and cooling nuclear reactors.

ACTIVITIES

The following activities will teach more about the content of salt in foods and its ability to conduct electricity.

THE SODIUM (Na) HUNT

Need: Salt container; various canned or bagged foods with nutritional information

Procedure: Look at the amount of sodium in each serving of the foods you normally eat: salt, chips, catsup, nuts, breads, milk, and more. List some of those food choices, and sodium amount, in the table.

¼ tsp salt	1 oz. chips	catsup				
440 mg						

SALT LIGHTS UP A BULB

Need: a 12-oz. jar filled with distilled water, salt, a teaspoon, 2 metal paper clips, 3 alligator wires, a 6V bulb on mount, a 9V battery, goggles, gloves, a well-ventilated room

1. Wear the safety goggles and gloves.

2. Hold each paper clip with an alligator clip and mount them on opposite sides inside the jar until they touch the water.

3. Complete the circuit with a 9V battery and 6V bulb.
   Does light go on? _____

4. Add 1 teaspoon of salt to the jar and stir well.
   Does the light go on? _____

Salt in water makes it a good conductor of electricity, which is why the light bulb goes on.

5. Interesting observations:

   a. Watch what is happening near the paper clips connected to:

   the negative (–) end of the battery _____

   _____

   the positive (+) end of the battery _____

   _____

As electricity flows, chemical reactions happen and two different gases are released near each clip: hydrogen and chlorine.

b. What color does the water turn after 60 seconds?

_____

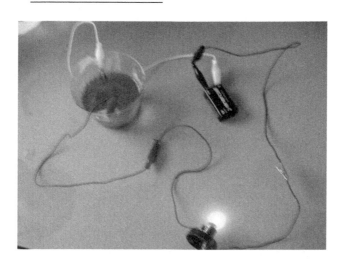

6. Disconnect the battery in a couple of minutes. The reaction will continue until the battery is depleted and the reaction has produced a green solution—which you should *not* drink! Discard the solution in a sink. Wash utensils with soap before you remove your gloves and goggles. After your gloves are off, wash your hands again well with soap.

This experiment, called electrolysis, was investigated by the same Michael Faraday (chapter two) who invented the electric generator. You will learn more on this when you take high school-level chemistry.

GOD'S LIGHT

Salt's power is also evident in the Bible. God used it to get His people's attention. It was a sign of His friendship and everlasting love, as well as a sign of covenant. There are more than thirty references to salt in the Bible. Let's look at a few.

1. Read **Exodus 30:35** to learn the ingredient God told Moses to mix with incense.

   "And make a fragrant blend of incense, the work of a perfumer. It is to be salted and pure and sacred."

Which ingredient made incense pure and holy?

_____

This incense was later burnt as an offering to honor God, who wants His children to worship Him forever.

2. Read **Leviticus 2:13.**

   "Season all your grain offerings with salt. Do not leave the salt of the covenant of your God out of your grain offerings; add salt to all your offerings."

God spoke to Moses to tell his people that they needed to add salt to their grain offerings.

This was to show _____ with God.

3. Read **2 Chronicles 13:5** to learn what one Jewish king told another in an effort to stop the war about to break out between them.

   "Don't you know that the LORD, the God of Israel, has given the kingship of Israel to David and his descendants forever by a covenant of salt?"

NOTES

God is promising that David's kingdom will be

_____. Salt was used as a symbol of

_____.

The genealogy of Jesus is found in Matthew 1:1-17 and Luke 3:23-37. Matthew lists the ancestors of Jesus through Joseph, and Luke lists them through Mary. So Jesus is a descendant of King David from the lineages of both his mother and father.

4. Read **Matthew 5:13-16.**

"You are the salt of the earth. But if the salt loses its saltiness, how can it be made salty again? It is no longer good for anything, except to be thrown out and trampled underfoot. You are the light of the world. A town built on a hill cannot be hidden. Neither do people light a lamp and put it under a bowl. Instead, they put it on its stand, and it gives light to everyone in the house. In the same way, let your light shine before others, that they may see your good deeds and glorify your Father in heaven."

- Jesus tells his followers that they are the _____ of the Earth and the _____ of the world.
- What happens to salt if it loses its saltiness?

  _____

- Is light any good if it is hidden?

  _____

- What does Jesus call his followers to do?

  _____ Why?

  _____

- Once you receive the light that is Jesus, what should you do?

  a. Keep it to yourself

  b. Share Him with the world

  c. Hide and tell no one

- You can be salt and light to others by (circle all that you believe are true):

  a. Explaining what Jesus did for them

  b. Saying that Jesus loves them

  c. Helping them in their need

  d. Tell them salvation is through Jesus

5. Read one of the last verses about salt, and then get to know Michael Faraday a little better. The verse is found in Colossians 4:6.

Let your conversation be always full of grace, seasoned with salt, so that you may know how to answer everyone.

Despite his great fame, Michael Faraday remained a devout Christian who shined the light of Jesus to those around him. He was humble and gentle and applied his faith at work, relying on prayer during difficult situations. His actions showed that he loved God and his fellow men; he was generous with his time and money. When invited to events by the noble class of England, even the Queen, he did not hesitate to assist someone in need instead. Here are two of Faraday's best quotations.

"The Bible, and it alone, with nothing added to it nor taken away from it by man, is the sole and sufficient guide for each individual, at all times and in all circumstances."

"Since peace is alone in the gift of God; and since it is He who gives it, why should we be afraid? His unspeakable gift in His beloved Son is the ground of no doubtful hope."

WHAT ARE YOU FOR CHRIST?

- Do you make life better for other people?

  _____

- List some ways you are willing to be salt and light to others.

  _____

  _____

  _____

  _____

MEMORY VERSE: MATTHEW 5:16

"In the same way, let your light shine before others, that they may see your good deeds and glorify your Father in heaven."

BIBLIOGRAPHY AND BOOK REFERENCES

1. R. Heddle and P. Shipton, *Science Activities: Volume Three* (Usborne Publishing, 1993), pp. 2, 18, 49.

2. Sally Hewitt, *Fascinating Science Projects: Light* (Aladdin Books Ltd., 2002), pp. 6, 7, 24.

3. H. Edom and K. Woodword, *Science Activities: Volume One* (Usborne Publishing), p. 25.

4. Phillip Eichman, *The Christian Character of Michael Faraday as Revealed in His Personal Life and Recorded Sermon Perspectives on Science and Christian Faith* 43 (June 1993), 92-95.

5. Charles Ludwig, "Michael Faraday, Father of Electronics," *Herald Press* (Scottsdale, Pa.), 1978.

6. Raymond J. Seeger, "Maxwell, Devout Inquirer" in *The Journal of the American Scientific Affiliation*, 37 (June 1985), pp. 93-96.

7. Dan Graves, *Scientists of Faith* (Kregel Resources, Grand Rapids MI, 1996), pp. 109-112, 150-153.

8. Mike Lynch, *Indiana Starwatch, The Essential Guide to Our Night Sky*, (Voyageur Press, 2006), p. 17.

9. Dr. Jonathan Henry, *The Astronomy Book* (Master Books, 1999, 2006).

10. Jeannie K. Fulbright, "Exploring Creation with Astronomy" (Apologia Educational Ministries, Inc., 2004).

11. National Maritime Museum, Greenwich, London: "Shadows and Sundials," http://certificate.ulo.ucl.ac.uk/modules/year_one/ROG/earth/shadows_sundials.html.

12. R. Heddle and P. Shipton, *Science Activities: Volume Three* (Usborne Publishing, 1993), p. 49.

13. *Life Application Study Bible NIV* (published by Tyndale and Zondervan), Commentary on John 14:6, p. 1911.

15. "The Sweet Meaning Behind Your Easter Candy," Trish Stukbauer, Catholic365.com, April 5, 2015.

16. Malcolm S. Longair, *Maxwell and the Science of Colour* (The Royal Society Publishing, May 28, 2008). DOI: 10.1098/rsta.2007.2178.

17. "Salt and Your Health, Part I: The Sodium Connection," Harvard Medical Groups, http://www.health.harvard.edu/newsletter_article/salt-and-your-health.

CPSIA information can be obtained
at www.ICGtesting.com
Printed in the USA
BVOW10s0728180517
484453BV00005B/7/P